BREAD MACHINE COOKBOOK FOR BEGINNERS

Simple Step-by-Step Recipes and Useful Insider Tips to Master the Art of Homemade Bakery-Quality Bread

Elizabeth E. Wright

Copyright© 2024 By Elizabeth E. Wright Rights Reserved

This book is copyright protected. It is only for personal use. You cannot amend, distribute, sell, use, quote or paraphrase any part of the content within this book, without the consent of the author or publisher.

Under no circumstances will any blame or legal responsibility be held against the publisher, or author, for any damages, reparation, or monetary loss due to the information contained within this book, either directly or indirectly.

Disclaimer Notice:

Please note the information contained within this document is for educational and entertainment purposes only. All effort has been executed to present accurate, up to date, reliable, complete information. No warranties of any kind are declared or implied. Readers acknowledge that the author is not engaged in the rendering of legal, financial, medical or professional advice. The content within this book has been derived from various sources. Please consult a licensed professional before attempting any techniques outlined in this book.

By reading this document, the reader agrees that under no circumstances is the author responsible for any losses, direct or indirect, that are incurred as a result of the use of the information contained within this document, including, but not limited to, errors, omissions, or inaccuracies.

Manufactured in the United States of America
Interior and Cover Designer: Danielle Rees
Art Producer: Brooke White
Editor: Aaliyah Lyons
Production Editor: Sienna Adams
Production Manager: Sarah Johnson
Photography: Michael Smith

TABLE OF CONTENTS

Introduction 1

Chapter 1: Embracing the Art of Homemade Bread 2

    Understanding Your Bread Machine.. 2

    Essential Ingredients for Bread Making.. 4

    Tips and Tricks for Perfect Bread 6

Chapter 2: Classic Daily Breads 8

    Wheat Bran Bread 9

    Butter Bread 9

    Golden Turmeric Cardamom Bread 10

    Dark Rye Bread 10

    Onion Loaf 10

    Yogurt Bread 11

    Basic Seed Bread 11

    Black Olive Bread 11

    Classic Dark Bread 12

    Easy Basic Vegan Bread 12

    Basil Oregano and Rosemary Bread 12

    Soft Egg Bread 13

    Oatmeal Walnut Bread 13

    Beer Bread 13

Chapter 3: Whole Grain & Specialty Flours 14

    Italian Whole Wheat Flatbread... 15

    Healthy Whole Wheat Challah 15

    Whole Wheat Rolls 16

    Whole Wheat Raisin Bread 16

    Potato Whole Wheat Bread 16

TABLE OF CONTENTS

    Brown Rice Flour Bread 17

    Honey Whole Wheat Bread 17

    Whole-Grain Daily Bread 17

    Coconut Flour Bread 18

    Molasses Wheat Bread 18

    Old-Fashioned Sesame-Wheat Bread 18

    100% Whole Wheat Bread 19

    Whole Wheat Maple Seed Bread 19

    Oatmeal Pecan Bread 19

Chapter 4: Sourdough & Country Loaves 20

    Sourdough Sandwich Bread 21

    Rustic Country Bread 21

    Sourdough Milk Bread 22

    Czech Sourdough Bread 22

    Sourdough Carrot Poppy Seed Bread 22

    Classic Sourdough Rye 23

    Crusty Sourdough Bread 23

    Multigrain Sourdough Bread 23

    Portuguese Sweet Gluten-Free Bread 24

    Country White Bread 24

    Sourdough Banana Nut Bread 24

    French Sourdough Bread 25

    Sourdough English Muffins 25

Chapter 5: Rolls, Buns & Pizza Crusts 26

    Texas Roadhouse Rolls 27

    Virginia Light Rolls 27

    Lemon and Poppy Buns 28

    Hot Cross Buns 28

TABLE OF CONTENTS

No-Knead Pizza Dough 29

Thin Crust Pizza Dough 29

Bread Rolls 29

Whole Meal Rolls 30

Classic Pepperoni Pizza 30

Sandwich Buns 30

Sun-Dried Tomato Rolls 31

Multigrain Pull-Apart Rolls 31

Homemade Slider Buns 32

Rosemary Garlic Dinner Rolls 32

Chapter 6: Gluten-Free Breads 33

Gluten-Free Cinnamon Raisin Bread 34

Gluten-free Sorghum Bread 34

Gluten-Free White Bread 34

Gluten-Free Potato Bread 35

Gluten-Free Mock Light Rye 35

Gluten-Free Peasant Bread 35

Gluten-Free Buttermilk White Bread 36

Gluten-free Potato and Chive Bread 36

Gluten-free Crusty Boule Bread 37

Gluten-Free Oat & Honey Bread 37

Seeded Gluten-Free Loaf 37

Grain-Free Chia Bread 38

Gluten-Free Ricotta Potato Bread 38

Gluten-Free Chickpea Rice And Tapioca Flour Bread 38

Chapter 7: Spice, Nut & Herb Breads 39

Sunflower Bread 40

Raisin Seed Bread 40

v

TABLE OF CONTENTS

Cumin Tossed Fancy Bread 40

Fragrant Herb Bread 41

Pumpkin Coconut Almond Bread 41

Chia Sesame Bread 41

Flaxseed Milk Bread 42

Date and Nut Bread 42

California Nut Bread 42

Cumin Bread 43

Turmeric Bread 43

Cracked Black Pepper Bread 43

Toasted Walnut Bread 44

Herbed Pesto Bread 44

Chapter 8: Vegetable and Fruit Breads 45

Beetroot Bread 46

Tomato Basil Bread 46

Sage and Onion Loaf 46

Pumpkin Raisin Bread 47

Pineapple Juice Bread 47

Zucchini Bread 47

Cranberry Orange Bread 48

Apple Spice Bread 48

Strawberry Shortcake Bread 49

Cinnamon & Dried Fruits Bread 49

Feta And Spinach Bread 49

Tomato Onion Bread 50

Plum Orange Bread 50

Chapter 9: Sweet & Savory Breads 51

Sweet Potato Bread 52

Peanut Butter Bread 52

TABLE OF CONTENTS

Chocolate Marble Cake 52

Blue Cheese Onion Bread 53

Jalapeño Corn Bread 53

Honey Bread 53

Sampler Hawaiian Sweet Loaf 54

Roasted Garlic and Dry Jack Bread 54

Cherry Chocolate Bread 54

Dutch Sugar Loaf 55

Cheese, Ham, and Chile Strata 55

Chocolate Oatmeal Banana Bread 56

Mozzarella Cheese And Salami Loaf 56

Chapter 10: No-Yeast Breads 57

Bourbon Nut Quick Bread 58

Golden Corn Bread 58

No-Yeast Whole-Wheat Sourdough Starter 58

Pumpkin Quick Bread 59

White And Dark Chocolate Tea Cake 59

Collagen Keto Gluten-Free Bread 59

Almond Quick Bread with Cardamom 60

Caramel Apple Quick Bread 60

Toasted Coconut Bread 61

Tropical Quick Bread 61

Whole Wheat Soda Bread 62

Citrus Cranberry Bread 62

Anadama Quick Bread 62

Chapter 11: Bread from Around the World 63

Russian Rye Bread 64

Italian Semolina Bread 64

Moroccan Khobz 64

TABLE OF CONTENTS

Crusty French Bread 65

German Butter Cake 65

Russian Black Bread 66

German Pumpernickel 66

Japanese Milk Bread 66

Portuguese Sweet Bread 67

Greek Easter Bread 67

Australian Damper 67

Indian Naan 68

Italian Pine Nut Bread 68

Appendix 1: Measurement Conversion Chart 69

Appendix 2: The Dirty Dozen and Clean Fifteen 70

Appendix 3: Index 71

INTRODUCTION

I've always been a bread lover. There's just something about the smell of freshly baked bread that makes my heart sing. Making my own bread is one of my favorite pastimes. I love experimenting with different flavors and ingredients to create loaves that my family and I can't get enough of. It's such a thrill to come up with a new recipe that everyone enjoys.

Even when I'm traveling abroad, my passion for bread doesn't take a break. I make it a point to try the local bread wherever I go. Each country has its unique twist on this staple food, and I find it incredibly inspiring. From French baguettes to Italian focaccia, and everything in between, I love tasting the world's bread. It not only expands my palate but also gives me fresh ideas to try out in my kitchen.

Years of home baking have really honed my skills. I've become pretty good at making all the traditional everyday breads. Whether it's a simple white loaf, a hearty whole grain, or a tangy sourdough, I've got it covered. But what I really enjoy is developing new flavors and combinations. Adding herbs, spices, fruits, or nuts can transform a basic bread recipe into something extraordinary. It's like a little adventure every time I bake.

Sharing my love for bread-making with others is something I truly enjoy. There's nothing quite like seeing someone else discover the joy of baking their own bread. It's a wonderful feeling to pass on tips and tricks that I've picked up over the years, and to see others light up when they create their perfect loaf.

I hope to connect with many more bread-making enthusiasts out there. Whether you're a seasoned baker or just starting out, there's always something new to learn and share in the world of bread. Let's keep baking and enjoying every slice!

DEDICATION

To Rachel, I just wanted to thank you again for the incredible birthday gift you gave me a few years back—a bread machine that has become my kitchen's MVP. I've used it countless times, and it's still going strong, helping me bake delicious bread with ease. Your thoughtful present has not only made my baking journey more enjoyable but also allowed me to create wonderful memories and flavors for my family. I'm so grateful for your kindness and generosity. Thank you for such a perfect and lasting gift!

CHAPTER 1: EMBRACING THE ART OF HOMEMADE BREAD

UNDERSTANDING YOUR BREAD MACHINE

So, you've got a bread machine, and you're ready to dive into the world of homemade bread. Great choice! Bread machines can be a baker's best friend, making the process easier and more consistent. Let's break down what you need to know to get the most out of your new kitchen gadget.

- **KEY COMPONENTS AND FEATURES**

THE BREAD PAN

The bread pan is where all the magic happens. This is where your ingredients come together to form a beautiful loaf of bread. It's typically removable for easy cleaning and has a non-stick coating to ensure your bread slides out effortlessly once it's done. You'll want to ensure it's securely placed in the machine before you start adding ingredients.

KNEADING PADDLE

The kneading paddle is the workhorse of your bread machine. This small, often metal piece is responsible for mixing and kneading the dough. It's designed to move the ingredients around the pan, ensuring they're thoroughly combined and the dough is properly kneaded to develop gluten, which is crucial for the bread's texture.

CONTROL PANEL

The control panel is where you'll manage your bread-making process. It typically includes buttons for different settings like bread type, crust darkness, and baking time. A digital display might show you the time remaining and the current stage of the bread-making process. Familiarizing yourself with the control panel can help you make the most of your machine's

EMBRACING THE ART OF HOMEMADE BREAD

features and customize your bread to your liking.

- **BREAD MACHINE SETTINGS AND FUNCTIONS**

BASIC/WHITE BREAD

The basic or white bread setting is the go-to option for most bread recipes. It's designed to handle standard white or whole wheat bread, ensuring the right balance of kneading, rising, and baking times to produce a delicious loaf with a soft interior and a golden crust.

WHOLE WHEAT

Whole wheat bread requires a different approach because whole wheat flour is denser and has more bran. This setting adjusts the kneading and rising times to give the dough more time to develop and rise, resulting in a lighter, fluffier loaf.

DOUGH SETTING

If you prefer to shape and bake your bread in a conventional oven, the dough setting is perfect. It handles the mixing, kneading, and initial rising for you. After the dough is ready, you can take it out, shape it as you like, and bake it in your oven. This setting is also great for making pizza dough, rolls, and other bread-based recipes.

- **HOW DOES THE BREAD MACHINE WORK?**

Understanding the inner workings of your bread machine can help you troubleshoot and tweak your baking process for better results.

ADDING INGREDIENTS

The first step is to add your ingredients to the bread pan. Typically, liquids go in first, followed by dry ingredients, with yeast added last. This layering method helps prevent the yeast from activating too soon, which can affect the rise and texture of your bread.

MIXING AND KNEADING

Once you start the machine, the kneading paddle begins to mix and knead the ingredients. This process is crucial because it develops the gluten in the dough, giving the bread its structure. The machine will handle this step automatically, ensuring consistent results every time.

RISING

After kneading, the dough needs time to rise. The machine keeps the dough at an optimal temperature for yeast fermentation, allowing it to expand. This stage can take anywhere from one to two hours, depending on the recipe and the machine's settings.

BAKING

Finally, the machine bakes the bread. The heating element ensures an even temperature, cooking the bread

CHAPTER 1

thoroughly and creating a lovely crust. Some machines allow you to adjust the crust darkness, so you can have a light, medium, or dark crust according to your preference.

ESSENTIAL INGREDIENTS FOR BREAD MAKING

Making bread at home can be a rewarding and tasty adventure. To get started, it's important to understand the essential ingredients that go into making a great loaf. Here, we'll break down the basics and explain their roles, giving you a solid foundation to start your bread-making journey.

- **THE BASICS: FLOUR, YEAST, WATER, AND SALT**

FLOUR

Flour is the backbone of any bread recipe. It provides the structure and texture that make bread what it is. The most common flour used in bread making is wheat flour, specifically bread flour, which has a higher protein content. This protein, gluten, is what gives bread its chewy texture and helps it rise. All-purpose flour can also be used, but it may produce a slightly different texture.

YEAST

Yeast is the magic ingredient that makes bread rise. It's a living organism that ferments the sugars in the flour, producing carbon dioxide gas. This gas gets trapped in the dough, causing it to expand and become airy. There are two main types of yeast used in bread making: active dry yeast and instant yeast. Active dry yeast needs to be dissolved in water before using, while instant yeast can be mixed directly with the dry ingredients.

WATER

Water is essential for hydrating the flour and activating the yeast. The temperature of the water is important – it should be warm, but not too hot, to help the yeast grow. Too cold, and the yeast won't activate; too hot, and you'll kill the yeast. Water also helps to dissolve the salt and sugar, distributing them evenly throughout the dough.

SALT

Salt is a crucial ingredient in bread making. It adds flavor, strengthens the gluten structure, and helps control the fermentation process. Without salt, your bread would taste flat and bland, and the yeast could become too active, resulting in a crumbly texture. It's usually added after the initial mixing to prevent it from coming into direct contact with the yeast too early, which can inhibit yeast activity.

- **EXPLORING DIFFERENT TYPES OF FLOUR**

BREAD FLOUR

Bread flour is high in protein, usually around 12-14%, which makes it ideal for bread making. The high protein content helps develop strong gluten, giving the bread its chewy texture and good rise. This is the go-to flour for most bread recipes.

ALL-PURPOSE FLOUR

All-purpose flour has a lower protein content, around 10-12%, making it more versatile for various baking needs. It can be used for bread, but the texture might be slightly less chewy compared to bread flour. It's a good option if you're looking for a softer loaf.

WHOLE WHEAT FLOUR

Whole wheat flour is made from the entire wheat kernel, including the bran and germ. It's higher in fiber and nutrients compared to white flour. However, it produces denser bread because the bran and germ can interfere with gluten development. Often, recipes will mix whole wheat flour with bread flour to achieve a balance of nutrition and texture.

SPECIALTY FLOURS

There are many other types of flours you can experiment with, such as rye flour, spelt flour, and oat flour. Each brings its unique flavor and texture to the bread. These flours are often used in combination with wheat flour to help maintain the bread's structure and rise.

- **THE ROLE OF YEAST AND HOW TO USE IT**

ACTIVE DRY YEAST

Active dry yeast is the most commonly used type of yeast in home baking. It comes in granules and needs to be dissolved in warm water before being added to the dough. This helps to "wake up" the yeast and get it ready for fermentation. To use it, dissolve the yeast in a small amount of water (about 100°F to 110°F) and let it sit for about 5-10 minutes until it becomes frothy.

INSTANT YEAST

Instant yeast, also known as rapid-rise or quick-rise yeast, can be mixed directly into the dry ingredients. It doesn't require proofing in water, which can save you a step. Instant yeast is more finely ground and works faster than active dry yeast, which can shorten the rising time. It's great for recipes where you want to speed up the bread-making process.

CHAPTER 1

FRESH YEAST

Fresh yeast, also known as cake yeast or compressed yeast, comes in a solid, crumbly block. It has a short shelf life and needs to be stored in the refrigerator. To use fresh yeast, crumble it into warm water and stir until it dissolves. It's less commonly used in home baking but can give bread a slightly different flavor and texture.

UNDERSTANDING YEAST ACTIVITY

The activity of yeast is influenced by several factors, including temperature, moisture, and sugar. Warm temperatures (around 75°F to 85°F) are ideal for yeast fermentation. Yeast also needs moisture to activate and sugar to feed on, which produces the carbon dioxide gas that makes the dough rise. However, too much sugar can dehydrate the yeast and too much salt can inhibit its activity. Balancing these elements is key to successful bread making.

TIPS AND TRICKS FOR PERFECT BREAD

Baking bread at home can be a fulfilling and delicious experience, but it comes with its own set of challenges. Here are some tips and tricks to help you achieve that perfect loaf every time, covering everything from measuring ingredients accurately to maintaining the right dough consistency and storing your bread properly.

- **MEASURING INGREDIENTS ACCURATELY**

USE A KITCHEN SCALE

One of the best ways to ensure your bread turns out perfectly every time is to measure your ingredients by weight rather than volume. Flour, in particular, can be tricky to measure consistently using cups because it can settle or be packed differently each time. A kitchen scale provides precise measurements, leading to more consistent results. For example, a cup of flour can weigh anywhere from 120 to 140 grams depending on how it's measured, but a scale will give you an exact number.

LEVEL YOUR INGREDIENTS

If you don't have a scale and need to measure by volume, make sure to level off your dry ingredients with a flat edge, like the back of a knife. This ensures you're not using too much flour, which can make your bread dense and dry. When measuring liquids, use a clear measuring cup and check the measurement at eye level to ensure accuracy.

BE MINDFUL OF HUMIDITY

Humidity can affect how much flour your dough needs. On a humid day, your flour might absorb more moisture from the air, making your dough stickier. Conversely, on a dry day, you might need to add a bit more water. Pay attention to the dough's feel and adjust as necessary.

- **BREAD STORAGE**

COOL COMPLETELY BEFORE STORING

It's tempting to dig into a fresh loaf of bread right away, but it's important to let it cool completely before storing it. This allows the interior to set properly and prevents excess moisture from making the crust soggy.

PROPER STORAGE METHODS

To keep your bread fresh, store it in a paper bag or bread box at room temperature. Plastic bags can make the crust soft and encourage mold growth. If you need to keep your bread for more than a couple of days, consider freezing it. Slice the bread first, so you can take out just what you need. Wrap it tightly in plastic wrap or aluminum foil, then place it in a freezer-safe bag. When you're ready to eat it, thaw the slices at room temperature or pop them straight into the toaster.

REVIVING STALE BREAD

If your bread starts to go stale, don't worry! You can easily revive it. Sprinkle the crust with a little water and place it in a 350°F oven for about 10-15 minutes. This will help to rehydrate the bread and crisp up the crust. Alternatively, you can make delicious croutons, bread pudding, or breadcrumbs with stale bread.

AVOID REFRIGERATION

While it might seem like a good idea to store bread in the fridge, it actually speeds up the staling process. The cool temperatures cause the starches in the bread to crystallize more quickly, leading to a dry, crumbly texture. Stick to room temperature storage for best results.

With these essential tips, you'll be well-equipped to bake perfect bread at home. Embrace the process, experiment, and enjoy the delicious rewards of your efforts. Happy baking!

CHAPTER 2: CLASSIC DAILY BREADS

CLASSIC DAILY BREADS

WHEAT BRAN BREAD

Prep time: **5 minutes** | Cook time: **1 hour** | Serves **4**

- 16 slice bread (2 pounds)
- 1½ cups lukewarm milk
- 3 tbsp unsalted butter, melted
- ¼ cup sugar
- 2 tsp table salt
- ½ cup wheat bran
- 3½ cups white bread flour
- 2 tsp bread machine yeast
- 12 slice bread (1½ pounds)
- 1⅛ cups lukewarm milk
- 2¼ tbsp unsalted butter, melted
- 3 tbsp sugar
- 1½ tsp table salt
- ⅓ cup wheat bran
- 2⅔ cups white bread flour
- 1½ tsp bread machine yeast

1. Choose the size of loaf you would like to make and measure your ingredients.
2. Add the ingredients to the bread pan in the order listed above.
3. Place the pan in the bread machine and close the lid.
4. Turn on the bread maker. Select the White/Basic setting, then the loaf size, and finally the crust color. Start the cycle.
5. When the cycle is finished and the bread is baked, carefully remove the pan from the machine. Use a potholder as the handle will be very hot. Let rest for a few minutes.
6. Remove the bread from the pan and allow to cool on a wire rack for at least 10 minutes before slicing.

BUTTER BREAD

Prep time: **10 minutes** | Cook time: **20 minutes** | Serves **4**

- 1 cup water
- 1 large egg
- 5 tbsp unsalted butter or margarine, cut into pieces
- 3 cups bread flour
- 1 tbsp gluten
- 1½ tsp salt
- 2 tsp SAF yeast or 2½ tsp bread machine yeast

1. Place all the ingredients in the pan according to the order in the manufacturer's instructions. Set crust on medium and program for the Basic or Variety cycle; press Start. (This recipe is not suitable for use with the Delay Timer.)
2. If you are using the Basic cycle, after Rise 1 ends press Pause, remove the bread from the machine, and close the lid. If you are using the Variety cycle, remove the pan when Shape appears in the display. Turn the dough out onto a clean work surface and divide it into 2 equal portions. Flatten each portion into a small rectangle and roll up from a short side to form 2 fat squares of dough. Remove the kneading blade and give the pan a light greasing by spraying it with a bit of vegetable cooking spray. Place the 2 separate pieces side by side in the bottom of the bread pan (they will be touching). Return the pan to the machine.
3. Press Start to continue to rise and bake as programmed. When the baking cycle ends, immediately remove the bread from the pan and place it on a rack. Let cool to room temperature before slicing.

CHAPTER 2

GOLDEN TURMERIC CARDAMOM BREAD

Prep time: **5 minutes** | Cook time: **3 hours** | Serves **12**

- 1 cup lukewarm water
- ⅓ cup lukewarm milk
- 3 tbsp butter, unsalted
- 3 ¾ cups unbleached all-purpose flour
- 3 tbsp sugar
- 1 ½ tsp salt
- 2 tbsp ground turmeric
- 1 tbsp ground cardamom
- ½ tsp cayenne pepper
- 1 ½ tsp active dry yeast

1. Add liquid ingredients to the bread pan.
2. Measure and add dry ingredients (except yeast) to the bread pan.
3. Make a well in the center of the dry ingredients and add the yeast.
4. Snap the baking pan into the bread maker and close the lid.
5. Choose the Basic setting, preferred crust color and press Start.
6. When the loaf is done, remove the pan from the machine. After about 5 minutes, gently shake the pan to loosen the loaf and turn it out onto a rack to cool.

DARK RYE BREAD

Prep time: **5 minutes** | Cook time: **10 minutes** | Serves **4**

- 12 slice bread (1½ pounds)
- 1 cup water, at 80°F to 90°F
- 1½ tbsp melted butter, cooled
- 1½ tbsp unsalted butter, melted
- ⅓ cup molasses
- ⅓ tsp salt
- 1½ tbsp unsweetened cocoa powder
- Pinch ground nutmeg
- ¾ cup rye flour
- 2 cups white bread flour
- 1⅔ tsp bread machine or instant yeast

1. Preparing the Ingredients.
2. Place the ingredients in your bread machine as recommended by the manufacturer.
3. Select the Bake cycle
4. Turn on the bread maker. Select the White / Basic setting, then select the dough size and crust color. Press start to start the cycle.
5. When this is done, and the bread is baked, remove the pan from the machine. Let stand a few minutes.
6. Remove the bread from the pan and leave it on a wire rack to cool for at least 10 minutes. Slice and serve.

ONION LOAF

Prep time: **5 minutes** | Cook time: **3 hours 40 minutes** | Serves **12**

- 1 tbsp butter
- 2 medium onions, sliced
- 1 cup water
- 1 tbsp olive or vegetable oil
- 3 cups bread flour
- 2 tbsp sugar
- 1 tsp salt
- 1 ¼ tsp bread machine or quick active dry yeast

1. Preheat a large skillet to medium-low heat and add butter to melt. Add onions and cook for 10 to 15 minutes, stirring often, until onions are brown and caramelized; remove from heat.
2. Add remaining ingredients, except onions, to the bread maker pan in the order listed above.
3. Select the Basic cycle, medium crust color, and press Start.
4. Add ½ cup of the onions 5 to 10 minutes before the last kneading cycle ends.
5. Remove baked bread from pan and allow to cool on a cooling rack before serving.

CLASSIC DAILY BREADS

YOGURT BREAD

Prep time: **10 minutes** | Cook time: **20 minutes** | Serves **4**

- ¾ cup water
- 1 cup plain whole milk yogurt
- 3½ cups bread flour
- 1 tbsp gluten
- 2 tsp salt
- 2 tsp SAF yeast or 2½ tsp bread machine yeast

1. Place all the ingredients in the pan according to the order in the manufacturer's instructions. I put 3¼ cups of flour in for the 1½ pound loaf (4½ cups for the 2-pound loaf) and sprinkle the rest in over the dough ball as needed, since yogurts have different consistencies.
2. Set crust on dark and program for the Basic cycle; press Start. (This recipe is not suitable for use with the Delay Timer.) The dough ball will be slightly sticky, but it will smooth out after the kneading.
3. When the baking cycle ends, immediately remove the bread from the pan and place it on a rack. Let cool to room temperature before slicing.

BASIC SEED BREAD

Prep time: **10 minutes** | Cook time: **10 minutes** | Serves **4**

- 12 slice bread (1½ pounds)
- 1⅛ cups lukewarm water
- 1½ tbsp unsalted butter, melted
- 1½ tbsp sugar
- 1⅛ tsp table salt
- 2½ cups white bread flour
- ¾ cup ground chia seeds
- 2 tbsp sesame seeds
- 1½ tsp bread machine yeast

1. Choose the size of bread to prepare. Measure and add the ingredients to the pan in the order as indicated in the ingredient listing. Place the pan in the bread machine and close the lid.
2. Close the lid, Turn on the bread maker. Select the White / Basic setting, then select the dough size, select light or medium crust. Press start to start the cycle.
3. When this is done, and the bread is baked, remove the pan from the machine. Let stand a few minutes.
4. Remove the bread from the skillet and leave it on a wire rack to cool for at least 10 minutes. Slice and serve.

BLACK OLIVE BREAD

Prep time: **10 minutes** | Cook time: **15 minutes** | Serves **4**

- 12 slices (1½ pounds)
- 1 cup milk, at 80°F to 90°F
- 1½ tbsp melted butter, cooled
- 1 tsp minced garlic
- 1½ tbsp sugar
- 1 tsp salt
- 3 cups white bread flour
- 1 tsp bread machine or instant yeast
- ⅓ cup chopped black olives

1. Choose the size of loaf of your preference and then measure the ingredients.
2. Add all of the ingredients mentioned previously in the list. Close the lid after placing the pan in the bread machine.
3. Turn on the bread machine. Select the White/Basic setting, select the loaf size, and the crust color. Press start.
4. When the cycle is finished, carefully remove the pan from the bread maker and let it rest.
5. Remove the bread from the pan, put in a wire rack to cool for at least 10 minutes.

CHAPTER 2

CLASSIC DARK BREAD

Prep time: **10 minutes** | Cook time: **10 minutes** | Serves **4**

- 12 slice bread (1½ pounds)
- 1 cup lukewarm water
- 1½ tbsp unsalted butter, melted
- ⅓ cup molasses
- ⅓ tsp table salt
- ¾ cup rye flour
- 2 cups white bread flour
- 2¼ cups whole-wheat bread flour
- 1½ tbsp unsweetened cocoa powder
- pinch ground nutmeg
- 1⅔ tsp bread machine yeast

1. Choose the size of bread to prepare. Measure and add the ingredients to the pan in the order as indicated in the ingredient listing. Place the pan in the bread machine and close the lid.
2. Close the lid, Turn on the bread maker. Select the White / Basic setting, then select the dough size and crust color. Press start to start the cycle.
3. When this is done, and the bread is baked, remove the pan from the machine. Let stand a few minutes.
4. Remove the bread from the skillet and leave it on a wire rack to cool for at least 10 minutes. Slice and serve.

EASY BASIC VEGAN BREAD

Prep time: **4 hours** | Cook time: **10 minutes** | Makes **2 lb loaf**

- 1 ½ cups water
- ⅓ cup Silk Soy Original
- 2 tbsp granulated sugar
- 2 tbsp canola oil
- 1 ½ tbsp salt
- 3 ½ cups all-purpose flour
- ¼ cup ground flax seeds
- 1 ½ tbsp bread machine yeast

1. In the sequence recommended by the manufacturer, add all of the to your bread machine.
2. For a 2-pound loaf, place the insert into the machine and select "basic cycle." If your machine has the option of crust color, always go with "medium brown." Take out the pan from the machine and put the loaf onto a cooling rack once the machine is finished (mine takes around 3 hours).
3. Then, before slicing, wait until the bread has completely cooled.
4. Because the loaf is still hot, its structure will be damaged during slicing, resulting in a squished loaf.
5. Slice your loaf lengthwise into two smaller loaves once it has cooled.
6. Cut these loaves into bread slices now.

BASIL OREGANO AND ROSEMARY BREAD

Prep time: **3 hours** | Cook time: **10 minutes** | Makes **1 ½ lb loaf**

- 1 cup warm water
- 1 egg (beaten)
- 1 tsp salt
- 2 tbsp white sugar
- 2 tbsp extra-virgin olive oil
- 2 tsp dried rosemary leaves (crushed)
- 1 tsp dried oregano
- 1 tsp dried basil
- 3 cup + 2 tbsp all-purpose flour
- 2 tsp bread machine yeast

1. Place the warm water in the bread machine pan.
2. Add the remaining to the manufacturer's recommended order.
3. Press Start after setting the machine to bake a big loaf with the Light Crust.
4. When the bake cycle ends, the bread is done.
5. Let your bread cool down before serving.

CLASSIC DAILY BREADS

SOFT EGG BREAD

Prep time: **5 minutes** | Cook time: **10 minutes** | Serves **4**

- 16 slice bread (2 pounds)
- 1 cup milk, at 80°F to 90°F
- 5 tbsp melted butter, cooled
- 3 eggs, at room temperature
- ⅓ cup sugar
- 2 tsp salt
- 4 cups white bread flour
- 1 cup oat bran
- 3 cups whole-wheat bread flour
- 1½ tsp bread machine or instant yeast

1. Preparing the Ingredients.
2. Place the ingredients in your bread machine as recommended by the manufacturer.
3. Select the Bake cycle
4. Turn on the bread maker. Select the White / Basic setting, then select the dough size and medium crust. Press Start.
5. When this is done, and the bread is baked, remove the pan from the machine. Let stand a few minutes.
6. Remove the bread from the pan and leave it on a wire rack to cool for at least 10 minutes. Slice and serve.

OATMEAL WALNUT BREAD

Prep time: **5 minutes** | Cook time: **1 hour and 30 minutes** | Serves **4**

- ¾ cup whole-wheat flour
- ¼ cup all-purpose flour
- ½ cup brown sugar
- ⅓ cup walnuts, chopped
- ¼ cup oatmeal
- ¼ tsp of baking soda
- 2 tbsp baking powder
- 1 tsp salt
- 1 cup Vegan buttermilk
- ¼ cup of vegetable oil
- 3 tbsp aquafaba

1. Add into the bread pan the wet ingredients then followed by the dry ingredients.
2. Use the "Quick" or "Cake" setting of your bread machine.
3. Allow the cycles to be completed.
4. Take out the pan from the machine.
5. Wait for 10 minutes, then remove the bread from the pan.
6. Once the bread has cooled down, slice it and serve.

BEER BREAD

Prep time: **10 minutes** | Cook time: **20 minutes** | Serves **4**

- 1 cup beer
- 2 tbsp olive oil
- 3½ cups bread flour
- ¼ cup sugar
- ¾ tsp salt
- 1¾ tsp SAF yeast or 2¼ tsp bread machine yeast

1. Pour the beer into a bowl and let stand at room temperature for a few hours to go flat.
2. Place all the ingredients in the pan according to the order in the manufacturer's instructions. Set crust on dark and program for the Basic cycle; press Start. (This recipe is not suitable for use with the Delay Timer.)
3. When the baking cycle ends, immediately remove the bread from the pan and place it on a rack. Let cool to room temperature before slicing.

CHAPTER 3: WHOLE GRAIN & SPECIALTY FLOURS

WHOLE GRAIN & SPECIALTY FLOURS

ITALIAN WHOLE WHEAT FLATBREAD

Prep time: **10 minutes** | Cook time: **25 to 30 minutes** | Serves **4**

- ⅔ cup water
- 1 cup milk
- 3 tbsp extra-virgin olive oil
- 3 cups unbleached all-purpose flour
- 1 cup whole wheat flour
- 2¼ tsp SAF yeast or 2¾ tsp bread machine yeast
- 3 to 4 tbsp extra-virgin olive oil, for drizzling
- 2 tsp coarse sea salt, for sprinkling

1. Place the dough ingredients in the pan according to the order in the manufacturer's instructions. Program for the Dough cycle; press Start. The dough will be soft, but still form a dough ball.
2. Brush a 15-by-10-by-1-inch metal jelly roll pan with olive oil. When the machine beeps at the end of the cycle, press Stop and unplug the machine. Immediately remove the bread pan and turn the dough out onto the prepared pan. Using the heel of your hand, press and flatten the dough to fit the pan. Cover gently with oiled plastic wrap and let rise at room temperature until doubled in bulk, about 1 hour.
3. Twenty minutes before baking, place a baking stone on the center rack of a cold oven and preheat it to 450°F.
4. Using your fingertips or knuckles, gently dimple the dough all over the surface. Drizzle the olive oil over the dough, letting it pool in the indentations. Reduce the oven temperature to 425°F. Bake for 25 to 30 minutes, or until nicely browned. Sprinkle the bread with the sea salt. Let cool for 10 minutes in the pan, then cut into squares, or slide onto a rack to cool.

HEALTHY WHOLE WHEAT CHALLAH

Prep time: **3 hours 5 minutes** | Cook time: **5 minutes** | Serves **One loaf**

- 1 cup water
- 3 large eggs
- 3 tbsp vegetable oil
- 2 tbsp honey
- 1 ½ cups whole wheat flour
- 1 ½ cup bread flour
- 1 ½ tbsp gluten
- 1 tbsp instant potato flake
- 1 ½ tsp salt
- 2 ½ tsp bread machine yeast

1. According to the order suggested by the manufacturer, place all in the pan. Set the medium or dark crust and the Basic or Whole Wheat cycle program; press Start. The dough's going to be moist. During kneading, do not add more flour, or the bread will dry.
2. Press Pause and then open the lid to check the dough by lifting it out of the pan when Rise 2 ends. Split the dough into two equal pieces. Roll each portion with the palms of your hands into a flat oblong sausage, about 10 inches in length.
3. Side by side, place the two pieces. Holding each end, wrapping one around the other, and simultaneously twisting each one to create a fat twist effect. Tuck the ends underneath and replace them in the machine pan. In the machine, the twisted form will bake.
4. Remove the bread from the pan when the baking cycle ends, and then place it on a rack to cool it on a rack before slicing.

CHAPTER 3

WHOLE WHEAT ROLLS

Prep time: **5 minutes** | Cook time: **3 hours** | Serves **12**

- 1 tbsp sugar
- 1 tsp salt
- 2 ¾ cups whole wheat flour
- 2 tsp dry active yeast
- ¼ cup water
- 1 egg
- 1 cup milk
- ¼ cup butter

1. All ingredients should be brought to room temperature before baking.
2. Add the wet ingredients to the bread maker pan.
3. Measure and add the dry ingredients (except yeast) to the pan.
4. Make a well in the center of the dry ingredients and add the yeast.
5. Carefully place the yeast in the hole.
6. Select the Dough cycle, then press Start.
7. Divide dough into 12 portions and shape them into balls.
8. Preheat an oven to 350°F. Place rolls on a greased baking pan.
9. Bake for 25 to 30 minutes, until golden brown.
10. Butter and serve warm.

WHOLE WHEAT RAISIN BREAD

Prep time: **2 ½ hours** | Cook time: **10 minutes** | Makes **1,5 lb loaf**

- 3 ½ cups Whole wheat flour
- 2 tsp dry yeast
- 2 eggs
- ¼ cup Butter
- ¾ cup water
- ⅓ cup Milk
- 1 tsp salt
- ⅓ cup Sugar
- 4 tsp Cinnamon
- 1 cup Raisins

1. In a bread pan, combine the water, milk, butter, and eggs.
2. Toss the other into the bread pan, excluding the yeast.
3. With your finger, make a small hole in the flour and pour the yeast into it.
4. Make certain that no liquids will come into contact with the yeast.
5. Start by selecting whole wheat and then light/medium crust.
6. Remove the loaf pan from the machine after the loaf is done.
7. Allow 10 minutes for cooling.
8. Cut into slices and serve.

POTATO WHOLE WHEAT BREAD

Prep time: **2 hours 45 minutes** | Cook time: **10 minutes** | Makes **2 lb loaf**

- 1⅔ cups water
- 4 tbsp butter
- 3 tbsp honey
- 2½ cups whole wheat flour
- 1½ cups bread flour
- ⅓ cup instant potato flakes
- 2 tbsp gluten
- 2 tsp salt
- 1 tbsp bread machine yeast

1. Place all of the in the pan in the sequence specified by the maker.
2. Set the crust to medium and select the Whole Wheat cycle from the menu; hit Start.
3. When the bake cycle ends, the bread is ready.
4. Please take the bread from the pan and place it on a rack when the baking cycle is finished.
5. Before slicing, allow it cool to room temperature.

WHOLE GRAIN & SPECIALTY FLOURS

BROWN RICE FLOUR BREAD

Prep time: **10 minutes** | Cook time: **20 minutes** | Serves **8**

- 1⅔ cups water
- 3 tbsp olive oil
- 3 tbsp honey
- 1¾ cups whole wheat flour
- 1¼ cups bread flour
- 1 cup brown rice flour
- 2 tbsp nonfat dry milk
- 2 tbsp gluten
- 2 tsp salt
- 1 tbsp plus 1 tsp SAF yeast or 1 tbsp plus 1½ tsp bread machine yeast

1. Place all the ingredients in the pan according to the order in the manufacturer's instructions. Set crust on dark and program for the Whole Wheat cycle; press Start. (This recipe may be made using the Delay Timer.)
2. When the baking cycle ends, immediately remove the bread from the pan and place it on a rack. Let cool to room temperature before slicing.

HONEY WHOLE WHEAT BREAD

Prep time: **10 minutes** | Cook time: **20 minutes** | Serves **4**

- ⅓ cup water
- ½ cup milk
- ¼ cup honey
- 1 large egg
- 1 tbsp butter, cut into pieces
- 2 cups bread flour
- 1 cup whole wheat flour
- 1 tbsp plus 1 tsp gluten
- 2 tsp salt
- 2¼ tsp SAF yeast or 2¾ tsp bread machine yeast

1. Place all the ingredients in the pan according to the order in the manufacturer's instructions. Set crust on medium and program for the Basic cycle; press Start. (This recipe is not suitable for use with the Delay Timer.)
2. When the baking cycle ends, immediately remove the bread from the pan and place it on a rack. Let cool to room temperature before slicing.

WHOLE-GRAIN DAILY BREAD

Prep time: **10 minutes** | Cook time: **20 minutes** | Serves **6**

- 1½ cups buttermilk
- 1 cup cooked whole grain of choice, firmly packed
- 3 tbsp canola oil
- 3 tbsp honey
- 3½ cups bread flour
- ⅔ cup whole wheat flour
- ½ cup rolled oats
- 1 tbsp plus 1 tsp gluten
- 2 tsp salt
- 2½ tsp SAF yeast or 1 tbsp bread machine yeast

1. Place all the ingredients in the pan according to the order in the manufacturer's instructions. Set crust on dark and program for the Basic cycle; press Start. (This recipe is not suitable for use with the Delay Timer.) Reach in and touch the dough with your fingers, being careful to avoid the rotating blade. The dough ball will be quite soft. Add another tbsp of flour if it is too sticky around the blade.
2. When the baking cycle ends, immediately remove the bread from the pan and place it on a rack. Let cool to room temperature before slicing.

CHAPTER 3

COCONUT FLOUR BREAD

Prep time: **3 ½ hours** | Cook time: **10 minutes** | Makes **1 lb loaf**

- ¾ cup warm water
- 1 ½ cups coconut flour
- 1 ½ cups bread flour
- 2 eggs
- 1 tsp salt
- 1 tsp baking powder
- ⅓ cup honey
- ⅓ cup vegetable oil
- ¼ cup oats (optional)
- ¼ cup coconut shredded (optional)
- 2 ½ tsp granulated yeast

1. Except for the yeast, put the dry in a small mixing dish.
2. Combine all of the wet in the bread machine pan.
3. Toss all of the dry into the bread machine pan from the small mixing dish.
4. Add the yeast on top.
5. Select the basic bread option on the bread maker.
6. Remove the bread machine pan from the bread machine once the bread is done.
7. Let it cool before transferring to a wire rack to cool completely.
8. The bread can be kept on the counter for up to four days and frozen for three months.

MOLASSES WHEAT BREAD

Prep time: **5 minutes** | Cook time: **10 minutes** | Serves **4**

- 12 slice bread (1½ pound)
- ¾ cup water, at 80°F to 90°F
- ⅓ cup milk, at 80°F
- 1 tbsp melted butter, cooled
- 3¾ tbsp honey
- 2 tbsp molasses
- 2 tsp sugar
- 2 tbsp skim milk
- powder
- ¾ tsp salt
- 2 tsp unsweetened cocoa powder
- 1¾ cups whole-wheat flour
- 1¼ cups white bread flour
- 1⅛ tsp bread machine yeast or instant yeast

1. Preparing the Ingredients.
2. Choose the size of bread to prepare. Measure and add the ingredients to the pan in the order as indicated in the ingredient listing. Place the pan in the bread machine and close the lid.
3. Select the Bake cycle
4. Turn on the bread maker. Select the White / Basic setting, then select the dough size and crust color. Press start to start the cycle.
5. When this is done, and the bread is baked, remove the pan from the machine. Let stand a few minutes.
6. Remove the bread from the pan and leave it on a wire rack to cool for at least 10 minutes.
7. After this time, proceed to cut it.

OLD-FASHIONED SESAME-WHEAT BREAD

Prep time: **10 minutes** | Cook time: **20 minutes** | Serves **4**

- ¾ cup water
- 3/8 cup milk
- 2 tbsp butter, cut into pieces
- 2¼ cups bread flour
- ¾ cup whole wheat flour
- 2 tbsp light or dark brown sugar
- 1 tbsp sesame seeds
- 1 tbsp plus 1 tsp gluten
- 1½ tsp salt
- 2 tsp SAF yeast or 2½ tsp bread machine yeast

1. Place all the ingredients in the pan according to the order in the manufacturer's instructions. Set crust on medium and program for the Basic cycle; press Start. (This recipe is not suitable for use with the Delay Timer.)
2. When the baking cycle ends, immediately remove the bread from the pan and place it on a rack. Let cool to room temperature before slicing.

WHOLE GRAIN & SPECIALTY FLOURS

100% WHOLE WHEAT BREAD

Prep time: 10 minutes | Cook time: 20 minutes | Serves 4

- ¾ cup water
- ¾ cup milk
- 2 tbsp canola oil
- ¼ cup light molasses
- 4 cups whole wheat flour
- 3 tbsp gluten
- 1¾ tsp salt
- 1 tbsp SAF yeast or 1 tbsp plus ½ tsp bread machine yeast

1. Place all the ingredients in the pan according to the order in the manufacturer's instructions. Set crust on medium and program for the Whole Wheat cycle; press Start. (This recipe is not suitable for use with the Delay Timer.)
2. When the baking cycle ends, immediately remove the bread from the pan and place it on a rack. Let cool to room temperature before slicing.

WHOLE WHEAT MAPLE SEED BREAD

Prep time: 3 hours | Cook time: 10 minutes | Makes 1 lb loaf

- ⅔ cup lukewarm water
- 1 tbsp olive oil
- 2 tbsp maple syrup
- 1¾ cups white whole wheat flour
- 6 tsp assorted seeds (an even mix of flax, sesame and sunflower seeds)
- ¾ tsp salt
- ¾ tsp instant yeast

1. Fill your bread maker with all of the in the precise sequence provided.
2. Select the whole-wheat setting and the medium crust function.
3. When the bake cycle ends, the bread is done, place it on a drying rack to cool before serving.

OATMEAL PECAN BREAD

Prep time: 2 ½ hours | Cook time: 10 minutes | Makes 1 ½ lb loaf

- 1 ¼ cups water
- ¼ cup molasses
- 1 tbsp vegetable oil
- 1 ½ tsp salt
- ½ cup dry oatmeal
- 1 cup whole wheat flour
- 2 ½ cups bread flour
- 2 tsp bread machine yeast
- ½ cup dried apricots (chopped)
- ⅓ cup pecans (chopped and toasted)

1. Add all in the bread pan in the order listed, except the apricots and pecans.
2. Securely place the bread pan in the baking chamber and close the cover.
3. Connect the item to a power source.
4. Choose WHOLE WHEAT.
5. Choose the size of the loaf and the color of the crust.
6. START/STOP by pressing the START/STOP button.
7. Add apricots and pecans at the "add ingredient" beep for larger loaves if adding directly to the bread pan.
8. When the bread is done, the entire signal will sound.
9. Remove the bread pan from the unit with potholders and carefully remove the bread from the pan. (If the kneading paddle is still in the bread, remove it once it has cooled.) Let the bread cool on a wire rack for at least 20 minutes before serving.

CHAPTER 4: SOURDOUGH & COUNTRY LOAVES

SOURDOUGH & COUNTRY LOAVES

SOURDOUGH SANDWICH BREAD

Prep time: 2 ½ hours | **Cook time: 10 minutes** | Makes **1 ½ lb loaf**

- 2 tbsp active dry yeast
- 2 cups Light Flour Blend
- ½ cup milk powder
- 3 tbsp granulated cane sugar
- 1 tbsp baking powder
- 2 tsp salt
- 1 tsp xanthan gum
- 1 cup sourdough starter (at room temperature)
- 4 tbsp unsalted butter (melted)
- 3 large eggs (beaten)
- ¼ cup water

1. In a small bowl, measure out the yeast and leave it aside.
2. Combine the remaining dry in a large mixing bowl.
3. Whisk the wet in a 4-cup glass measuring cup and pour into the bread pan.
4. Spread the dry over the wet components with a spatula.
5. Pour the yeast into a shallow well in the center.
6. Insert the bread pan into the machine, center it, and lock it in place.
7. Close the lid and choose from the following options: Cycle of Gluten-Free; Loaf size: 1 ½ pound; Medium crust.
8. Remove the bread pan from the machine and place it on a wire cooling rack on its side.
9. Allow for a few minutes in the pan before turning it upside down and sliding the loaf onto the wire rack.
10. If the paddle is stuck in the bottom of the bread, remove it before slicing, cool the loaf upside down for at least 2 hours.

RUSTIC COUNTRY BREAD

Prep time: 30 minutes | **Cook time: 16 hours 40 minutes** | Serves **12**

- ¾ cup spring water
- ¼ tsp. bread machine yeast
- 1 ¾ cups bread flour
- 1 cup spring water
- ½ tsp. bread machine yeast
- 2 cups bread flour
- ⅓ cup whole wheat flour
- ¼ tsp. salt

1. 1 day before preparing the bread, into bread machine pan, add the following in this order ¾ cup of spring water, ¼ tsp. of bread machine yeast and 1 ¾ cup of bread flour. Use the dough cycle and leave to knead for five minutes. Press stop button on machine and allow to rise overnight.
2. The following day, into a non-metallic container, add the starter from the bread machine pan. For this recipe, save 1/3 cup and put the remainder in a freezer for later use.
3. Combine 1 cup of spring water, 1/3 cup of reserved starter, whole wheat flour, and ½ tsp. of yeast, salt, and 2 cups of bread flour together in a large bowl. Use the Dough Cycle and start the machine. Once ten 10 minutes elapse, take out the dough from the machine and transfer to a bowl that is lightly oiled. Use a damp towel to cover and allow to rise for about two hours until doubled. Then deflate the dough and allow to rise once again for about an hour until doubled.
4. Onto a surface that is lightly floured, turn out the dough and shape into a round loaf. Transfer the loaf into a baking sheet drizzled with cornmeal. Cover the loaf and allow to rise for about 40 minutes until almost doubled. In the meantime, preheat the oven to 200 degrees C (400 degrees F).
5. Use water to spray the loaf and put in the oven preheated. Spritz the loaf again after every 2 minutes during the first ten minutes of baking process. Then bake for around 40 minutes until you hear a hollow sound when you tap the loaf's bottom.

CHAPTER 4

SOURDOUGH MILK BREAD

Prep time: 3 hours 10 minutes | Cook time: 5 minutes | Serves 6-8

- 4 tbsp of sugar
- 4 cups of bread flour
- 1 ¼ tsp of salt
- 1 ½ cups of sour milk or regular milk
- 1 ¾ tsp of active dry yeast
- 1 ½ tbsp of oil

1. If using sour milk, you can make it by adding 1 tbsp of vinegar to 1 cup of room temperature milk. Let it rest for five minutes.
2. Put all the require din the container of the bread machine in the suggested order by the manufacturer.
3. Select a basic setting, medium crust. Press the start button.
4. Check dough after 5-10 minutes of kneading, add 1 tbsp of water or flour if the dough is too dry or too wet, respectively.

CZECH SOURDOUGH BREAD

Prep time: 15 minutes | 1 week (Starter) | Cook time: 3 hours | Serves 1 loaf

- 1 cup non-dairy milk
- 1 tbsp salt
- 1 tbsp honey
- 1 cup sourdough starter
- 1 ½ cups rye flour
- 1 cup bread flour
- ¾ cup wheat flour
- 1 ½ cup grated half-baked potato
- 5 tbsp wheat gluten
- 2 tsp caraway seeds

1. Add ingredients to the bread machine pan.
2. Choose the cycle of the dough.
3. The dough should rise, up to 24 hours, in the bread machine until it doubles in size. After rising, bake in the bread machine for one hour.

SOURDOUGH CARROT POPPY SEED BREAD

Prep time: 3 hours 40 minutes | Cook time: 5 minutes | Serves 6-8

- ¾ cup sourdough starter
- ½ cup buttermilk
- 1 ½ tbsp olive or walnut oil
- 2 ½ cups bread flour
- ½ cup whole wheat flour
- 1 ¼ cups shredded raw carrots
- 2 tbsp minced dried apricots
- 1 tbsp poppy seed
- 1 tbsp sugar
- 1 ½ tsp salt
- 1 ¼ tsp SAF yeast or 1 ¾ tsp bread machine yeast

1. Place all the in the pan according to the order in the manufacturer's instructions. Set crust on dark and program for the Basic cycle; press Start.
2. When the baking cycle ends, immediately remove the pan's bread and place it on a rack. Let cool to room temperature before slicing.

SOURDOUGH & COUNTRY LOAVES

CLASSIC SOURDOUGH RYE

Prep time: **5 minutes** | Cook time: **10 minutes** | Serves **6**

For the Sponge:
- 1 cup Next-Day Rye Sourdough Starter
- 1½ cups water
- 1½ cups light or medium rye flour
- ½ tsp SAF or bread machine yeast

For the Dough:
- 1½ tbsp unsalted butter, melted
- 3 cups bread flour
- 1½ tbsp sugar
- 1 tbsp plus 1 tsp caraway seeds
- 2 tsp salt
- 1¼ tsp SAF yeast or 1¾ tsp bread machine yeast

1. To make the sponge, place the sponge ingredients in the bread pan. Program for the Dough cycle; press Start. When the machine beeps at the end of the cycle, press Stop and unplug the machine. Let the sponge starter sit in the machine for 8 hours, or as long as overnight.
2. To make the dough, place all the dough ingredients in the bread pan with the sponge according to the order in the manufacturer's instructions. Set crust on medium and program for the Basic or French Bread cycle; press Start. (This recipe is not suitable for use with the Delay Timer.) The dough ball will be moist, tacky, and smooth.
3. When the baking cycle ends, immediately remove the bread from the pan and place it on a rack. Let cool to room temperature before slicing.

CRUSTY SOURDOUGH BREAD

Prep Time: **10 Minutes or Less** | Cooking time: **20 minutes** | Serves **4**

- ⅔ cup Simple Sourdough Starter, fed, active, and at room temperature
- ⅓ cup water, at 80°F to 90°F
- 4 tsp honey
- 1 tsp salt
- 2 cups white bread flour
- ¾ tsp bread machine or instant yeast
- 1 cup Simple Sourdough Starter, fed, active, and at room temperature
- ½ cup water, at 80°F to 90°F
- 2 tbsp honey
- 1½ tsp salt
- 3 cups white bread flour
- 1 tsp bread machine or instant yeast
- 1⅓ cups Simple Sourdough Starter, fed, active, and at room temperature
- ⅔ cup water, at 80°F to 90°F
- 2⅔ tbsp honey
- 2 tsp salt
- 4 cups white bread flour
- 1⅓ tsp bread machine or instant yeast

1. Place the ingredients in your bread machine as recommended by the manufacturer.
2. Program the machine for Basic/White bread, select light or medium crust, and press Start.
3. When the loaf is done, remove the bucket from the machine.
4. Let the loaf cool for 5 minutes.
5. Gently shake the bucket to remove the loaf, and turn it out onto a rack to cool.

MULTIGRAIN SOURDOUGH BREAD

Prep time: **10 minutes** | Cook time: **45 minutes** | Serves **10**

- ⅓ cup plus 1 tbsp hot water
- ½ cup simple sourdough starter, fed, active, and at room temperature
- 4 tsp melted butter, cooled
- 1⅔ tbsp sugar
- ½ tsp salt
- 1 tsp bread machine yeast
- ½ cup multigrain cereal
- 1¾ cups bread flour (white)

1. Put all ingredients in the bread machine.
2. Program the machine for Whole-Wheat/Whole-Grain bread, select light or medium crust, and press Start.
3. When ready, remove the bread and allow about 5 minutes cooling the loaf.
4. Put it on a rack to cool it completely.

CHAPTER 4

PORTUGUESE SWEET GLUTEN-FREE BREAD

Prep time: 10 minutes | Cook time: 3 hours | Serves 6

Dry:
- 3 cups self-rising gluten-free flour
- ⅓ cup sugar
- 2 tbsp margarine
- ¾ tsp salt

Wet
- 1 egg
- 1 cup milk

1. Add the egg and milk first into the bread pan before adding the other ingredients.
2. Set the bread machine to "Normal" or "Basic" with a medium crust setting.
3. Wait until the cycles are finished.
4. Remove the bread from the machine to cool it down.
5. Slice and serve.

COUNTRY WHITE BREAD

Prep time: 3 hours | Cook time: 45 minutes | Serves 2 loaves

- 2 tsp active dry yeast
- 1 ½ tbsp sugar
- 4 cups bread flour
- 1 ½ tsp salt
- 1 large egg
- 1 ½ tbsp butter
- 1 cup warm milk, with a temperature of 110°F to 115°F

1. Put all the liquid ingredients in the pan. Add all the dry ingredients, except the yeast. Use your hand to form a hole in the middle of the dry ingredients. Put the yeast in the hole.
2. Secure the pan in the chamber and close the lid. Choose the basic setting and your preferred crust color. Press Start.
3. Once done, transfer the baked bread to a wire rack. Slice once cooled.

SOURDOUGH BANANA NUT BREAD

Prep time: 10 minutes | Cook time: 10 minutes | Serves 4

- ¾ cups sourdough starter
- ½ cup buttermilk
- ⅔ cup sliced bananas
- 1 large egg
- 3 tbsp nut oil
- 3⅓ cups bread flour
- ⅔ cup whole wheat flour
- ⅔ cup chopped macadamia nuts or pecans
- 4 tbsp chopped dried pineapple or dates
- 3 tbsp light brown sugar
- 1½ tsp salt
- 2¼ tsp SAF yeast or 2¾ tsp bread machine yeast

1. Place all the ingredients in the pan according to the order in the manufacturer's instructions. Set crust on medium and program for the Basic cycle; press Start. (This recipe is not suitable for use with the Delay Timer.)
2. When the baking cycle ends, immediately remove the bread from the pan and place it on a rack. Let cool to room temperature before slicing.

SOURDOUGH & COUNTRY LOAVES

FRENCH SOURDOUGH BREAD

Prep time: 15 minutes | 1 week (starter) | **Cook time:** 3 hours | **Serves** 2 loaf

- 2 cups sourdough starter
- 1 tsp salt
- ½ cup water
- 4 cups white bread flour
- 2 tbsp white cornmeal

1. Add the ingredients to the bread machine pan, saving cornmeal for later.
2. Choose the dough cycle.
3. Conventional Oven:
4. Preheat oven to 375°F.
5. At the end of the dough cycle, place dough onto a surface that is floured.
6. Add flour if the dough is sticky.
7. Divide dough into 2 portions and flatten it into an oval shape 1½ inch thick.
8. Fold ovals in half lengthwise and pinch seams to elongate.
9. Sprinkle cornmeal onto the baking sheet and place the loaves seam side down.
10. Cover and let it rise in until is about in doubled.
11. Place a deep pan of hot water on the bottom shelf of the oven
12. Use a knife to make shallow, diagonal slashes in the top of the loaves
13. Place the loaves in the oven and sprinkle with fine water. Spray the oven walls as well.
14. Repeat spraying 3 times at one-minute intervals.
15. Remove the pan of water after 15 minutes of baking
16. Fully bake for 30 to 40 minutes or until golden brown.

SOURDOUGH ENGLISH MUFFINS

Prep time: 10 minutes | **Cook time:** 10 minutes | **Serves** 4

- 1 cup sourdough starter
- ½ cup fat-free milk
- 2 tbsp unsalted butter, melted
- 1 large egg
- 3¾ cups bread flour
- 1½ tsp salt
- 2 tsp SAF yeast or 2½ tsp bread machine yeast
- ⅓ cup yellow cornmeal or coarse semolina, for sprinkling

1. Place all the ingredients in the pan according to the order in the manufacturer's instructions. Program for the Dough cycle; press Start. The dough ball will be soft and very slightly moist. The softer you leave the dough, the lighter the muffin will be. You can add a bit more flour when you remove the dough from the machine.
2. Lightly sprinkle the work surface with cornmeal. When the machine beeps at the end of the cycle, using a dough card scrape the dough out onto the work surface and, with a rolling pin, roll it into a rectangle about ½-inch thick. Sprinkle the top with cornmeal to prevent sticking. Cut out the muffins with a 3-inch biscuit cutter or the rim of a drinking glass. Roll out the scraps and cut out the remaining muffins. Cover the muffins with a clean tea towel or place them in the refrigerator if they are rising too fast while the others are baking.
3. Preheat an electric griddle to 350° or 375°F, or heat a cast-iron griddle over medium heat until a drop of water sprinkled on the griddle dances across the surface. Lightly grease the surface. Place several muffins on the hot griddle. Cook for about 10 minutes on each side, turning when they are quite brown. English muffins take time to bake all the way through, and will swell and be very puffy while baking. Remove the muffins from the griddle with a spatula and cool on a rack.

25

CHAPTER 5: ROLLS, BUNS & PIZZA CRUSTS

ROLLS, BUNS & PIZZA CRUSTS

TEXAS ROADHOUSE ROLLS

Prep time: **5 minutes** | Cook time: **20 minutes** | Serves **18**

- ¼ cup warm water (80°F - 90°F)
- 1 cup warm milk (80°F -90°F)
- 1 tsp salt
- 1½ Tbsp butter + more for brushing
- 1 egg
- ¼ cup sugar
- 3½ cups unbleached bread flour
- 1 envelope dry active yeast

For Texas Roadhouse Cinnamon Butter:
- ½ cup sweet, creamy salted butter, softened
- ⅓ cup confectioners' sugar
- 1 tsp ground cinnamon

1. Add each ingredient to the bread machine in the order and at the temperature recommended by your bread machine manufacturer.
2. Select the dough cycle and press start.
3. Once cycle is done, transfer your dough onto a lightly floured surface.
4. Roll out the rectangle, fold it in half. Let it rest for 15 minutes.
5. Cut the roll into 18 squares. Transfer them onto a baking sheet.
6. Bake at 350°F in a preheated oven for 10-15 minutes.
7. Remove dough from the oven and brush the top with butter.
8. Beat the softened butter with a mixer to make it fluffy. Gradually add the sugar and cinnamon while blending. Mix well.
9. Take out the rolls, let them cool for 2-3 minutes.
10. Spread them with cinnamon butter on the top while they are warm.

VIRGINIA LIGHT ROLLS

Prep time: **10 minutes** | Cook time: **20 minutes** | Serves **16**

- 1 cup plus 1 tbsp milk
- 3 tbsp honey
- 2 large eggs
- 6 tbsp butter or margarine, cut into pieces
- 4¼ cups unbleached all-purpose flour
- 1½ tsp salt
- 2 tsp SAF yeast or 2½ tsp bread machine yeast
- 4 tbsp melted butter or margarine, for brushing

1. Place all the ingredients in the pan according to the order in the manufacturer's instructions. Program for the Dough cycle; press Start. The dough ball will be soft, but add no more than 2 to 3 extra tbsp of flour, as needed, if you think it necessary.
2. Line a large baking sheet with parchment paper. When the machine beeps at the end of the cycle, press Stop and unplug the machine. Turn the dough out onto a lightly floured surface. Divide the dough in half, then roll each half into a 2- to 3-inch cylinder. With a metal dough scraper or a chef's knife, cut the cylinder into 8 equal portions. Repeat with the second cylinder, making a total of 16 equal portions. Shape each portion like a miniature loaf by patting it into an oval, then rolling up from a short side to make a small compact cylinder about 4 inches long. Place the rolls in two rows of 8 with their long sides touching. Brush some melted butter on the tops of the rolls. Cover loosely with plastic wrap and let rise at room temperature until doubled in bulk, about 45 minutes.
3. Twenty minutes before baking, preheat the oven to 375°F.
4. Place the baking sheet in the center of the oven and bake for 25 to 28 minutes, until golden brown. Remove the rolls from the pan and cool on a rack. Serve warm, or cool to room temperature and reheat.

CHAPTER 5

LEMON AND POPPY BUNS

Prep time: **2 hours 50 minutes** | Cook time: **45 minutes** | Makes **10- 20 buns**

- melted butter for grease
- 1 and ⅓ cups hot water
- 3 tbsp powdered milk
- 2 tbsp crisco shortening
- 1 and ½ tsp salt
- 1 tbsp lemon juice
- 4 and ¼ cups bread flour
- ½ tsp nutmeg
- 2 tsp grated lemon rind
- 2 tbsp poppy seeds
- 1 and ¼ tsp yeast
- 2 tsp wheat gluten

1. Add all of the ingredients to your Bread Machine (except melted butter).
2. Set the program to "Dough" cycle and let the cycle run.
3. Remove the dough (using lightly floured hands) and carefully place it on a floured surface.
4. Cover with a light film/cling paper and let the dough rise for 10 minutes.
5. Take a large cookie sheet andgrease with butter.
6. Cut the risen dough into 15-20 pieces and shape them into balls.
7. Place the balls onto the sheet (2 inches apart) and cover.
8. Place in a warm place and let them rise for 30-40 minutes until the dough doubles.
9. Preheat your oven to 375 degrees F, transfer the cookie sheet to your oven and bake for 12-15 minutes. Brush the top with a bit of butter, enjoy!

HOT CROSS BUNS

Prep time: **10 minutes** | Cook time: **15 minutes** | Serves **4**

Dough

- 2 eggs plus enough water to equal 2 cups
- ½ cup butter, softened
- 4 cups bread flour
- ¾ tsp ground cinnamon
- ¼ tsp ground nutmeg
- 1½ tsp salt
- 2 tbsp granulated sugar
- 1½ tsp bread machine or fast-acting dry yeast
- ½ cup raisins
- ½ cup golden raisins
- 1 egg
- 2 tbsp cold water

Icing

- 1 cup powdered sugar
- 1 tbsp milk or water
- ½ tsp vanilla

1. Measure carefully, placing all dough ingredients except raisins, 1 egg and the cold water in bread machine pan in the order recommended by the manufacturer. Add raisins at the Raisin/Nut signal.
2. Select Dough/Manual cycle. Do not use delay cycle. Remove dough from pan, using lightly floured hands. Cover and let rest 10 minutes on lightly floured surface. Grease cookie sheet or 2 (9-inch) round pans. Divide dough in half. Divide each half into 8 equal pieces. Shape each piece into a smooth ball. Place balls about 2 inches apart on cookie sheet or 1 inch apart in pans. Using scissors, snip a cross shape in top of each ball. Cover and let rise in warm place about 40 minutes or until doubled in size.
3. Heat oven to 375°F. Beat egg and cold water slightly; brush on buns. Bake 18 to 20 minutes or until golden brown. Remove from cookie sheet to cooling rack. Cool slightly.
4. In small bowl, mix all icing ingredients until smooth and spreadable. Make a cross on top of each bun with icing.

ROLLS, BUNS & PIZZA CRUSTS

NO-KNEAD PIZZA DOUGH

Prep time: **5 minutes** | Cook time: **2 hours** | Serves **2**

- 4 cups flour
- 1½ tsp instant yeast
- 1½ tsp salt
- 1½ cups lukewarm water
- 1 tsp olive oil

1. Add the salt, flour, and yeast into the stand mixer bowl fitted with a paddle attachment. Mix for 1-2 minutes at a low speed. Pour all of the water into the bowl and mix for 1-2 minutes until you get a dough that doesn't stick to the sides.
2. You don't have to knead the dough. It should be soft and sticky without any flour streaks on the surface.
3. You can also mix the dough with your hands or using a wooden spoon in a large bowl, just follow these steps.
4. Grease a large mixing bowl with oil. Flour your hands and form a ball from the dough. Transfer it to the greased bowl and turn it a few times to coat it with oil.
5. Cover with plastic wrap and leave it for 2-3 hours to double in size.
6. When the dough has risen, it's ready to use for making pizza. You can put into the fridge for up to 2 days for further use. Remember to let it warm to room temperature for 1 hour before shaping.

THIN CRUST PIZZA DOUGH

Prep time: **1 ½ hour** | Cook time: **10 minutes** | Makes **1 lb loaf**

- ¾ cup warm water
- 2 cups all-purpose flour
- ½ tsp salt
- ¼ tsp white sugar
- 1 tsp active dry yeast
- 2 tsp olive oil

1. Pour the heated water into the bread machine's pan, and then sprinkle the flour on top.
2. Season with salt and sugar, and then add the yeast.
3. Push the start button on the machine and select the dough setting.
4. Transfer the dough to a well-floured surface when the machine says it's done.
5. Preheat the oven to 425 degrees Fahrenheit.
6. Roll or stretch the dough into a 14-inch-wide thin crust.
7. Keep the dough thick around the edges and brush it with olive oil.
8. Bake for 5 minutes in a preheated oven before removing to top with selected seasonings and finishing baking for about 15 minutes more.

BREAD ROLLS

Prep time: **20 minutes** | Cook time: **10 minutes** | Serves **5**

- 1 tsp xanthan gum
- ½ tsp salt
- 1 cup almond flour
- ¼ cup butter, melted
- ¾ cup keto protein powder
- 4 tbsp hot water
- 1 ½ tsp baking powder

1. Add all ingredients to the Bread Machine.
2. Select dough:setting. When the time is over, transfer the dough to the floured surface. Shape it into a ball and cut it into about 5 even pieces.
3. Line a cookie sheet with parchment paper.
4. Transfer rolls to a lined cookie sheet & bake for about 10-12 minutes at 375°F until golden brown.

CHAPTER 5

WHOLE MEAL ROLLS

Prep time: one hour and 35 minutes | **Cook time: 5 minutes** | **Serves 10**

- 1 tsp easy bake yeast
- 2 ¾ cups strong whole meal flour, plus extra for dusting
- 1 ¼ tsp fine sea salt
- two tsp malt extract
- 1 tbsp olive oil
- 1 ¾ cups of water (or half water and half milk)

1. Add all the into the pan in the correct order for your machine.
2. Fit the pan into the bread machine and close the lid.
3. Select the whole wheat dough setting and the size. Press Start.
4. When the program has finished, turn the dough onto a floured surface and knead lightly, knocking out the air until smooth.
5. Cut the dough into ten pieces and, keeping the surface floured, shape into rolls, flattening them slightly to look like baps. Arrange, smooth side up, and spaced about 2.5cm/1 in apart on an oiled baking sheet.
6. Cover with oiled film and leave to rise until doubled in size.
7. Meanwhile, preheat the oven to 200°C (Fan 180°C), 400°F, Gas 6.
8. Remove the film and dust the rolls with a little extra flour.
9. Put into the hot oven and cook for 15-20 minutes until golden brown and cooked through.
10. Transfer to a wire rack and leave to cool.

CLASSIC PEPPERONI PIZZA

Prep time: 10 minutes | **Cook time: 14 to 18 minutes** | **Serves 4**

- makes one 14-inch pizza
- 1 recipe pizza dough of choice
- 1 cup essential tomato-herb pizza sauce
- 4 ounces pepperoni, peeled and thinly sliced
- 1 cup shredded provolone cheese (4 ounces)
- 6 ounces mozzarella cheese, thinly sliced
- ¼ pound fresh mushrooms, sliced
- 1 green bell pepper, seeded and cut into rings
- olive oil, for drizzling

1. Twenty to thirty minutes before baking, place baking tiles or a pizza stone on the lowest rack of a cold oven and preheat it to 450° to 500°F. Brush a 14-inch pizza pan with olive oil and sprinkle with cornmeal or semolina.
2. Place the dough on a lightly floured work surface. Using the heel of your hand, press to flatten it. Roll out the dough in a circle, then lift it onto the pan and gently pull and press it into a circle to fit the pan. Shape a ½-inch rim around the edge of the crust.
3. Spread the dough with the tomato sauce, leaving a ½-inch border. Dot with pepperoni slices. Lay the cheeses over the top. Top with the mushrooms and peppers. Drizzle with olive oil.
4. Place the pizza pan on the hot stone and bake for 14 to 18 minutes, or until the dough is crisp and brown. Remove from the oven and slide the pizza off the pan onto a cutting board. Cut into wedges immediately with a chef's knife or pizza wheel and serve.

SANDWICH BUNS

Prep time: 10 minutes | **Cook time: 25 minutes** | **Serves 8**

- 4 eggs
- 2 ½ ounces almond flour
- 1 tbsp coconut flour
- 1 ounce psyllium
- 1 ½ cups eggplant, finely grated, juices drained
- 3 tbsp sesame seeds
- 1 ½ tsp baking powder
- Salt to taste

1. Whisk eggs until foamy, and then add grated eggplant.
2. In a separate bowl, mix all dry ingredients.
3. Add them to the egg mixture. Mix well.
4. Line a baking sheet with parchment paper and shape the buns with your hands.
5. Bake at 374°F for 20 to 25 minutes.

ROLLS, BUNS & PIZZA CRUSTS

SUN-DRIED TOMATO ROLLS

Prep time: **10 minutes** | Cook time: **65 minutes** | Serves **4**

- ¾ cup warm milk (105°F to 115°F)
- 2 cups bread flour
- ¼ cup chopped sun-dried tomatoes in oil, drained,
- 1 tbsp oil reserved
- 1 tbsp sugar
- 1 tsp salt
- 1½ tsp bread machine yeast

1. Measure carefully, placing all ingredients in bread machine pan in the order recommended by the manufacturer.
2. Select Dough/Manual cycle. Do not use delay cycle.
3. Remove dough from pan; place on lightly floured surface. Cover and let rest 10 minutes Lightly grease cookie sheet with shortening or spray with cooking spray.
4. Gently push fist into dough to deflate. Divide dough into 12 equal pieces. Shape each piece into a ball. Place balls about 2 inches apart on cookie sheet. Cover and let rise in warm place 30 to 45 minutes or until almost doubled in size.
5. Heat oven to 350°F. Bake 12 to 16 minutes or until golden brown. Remove from cookie sheet to cooling rack. Serve warm or cool.

MULTIGRAIN PULL-APART ROLLS

Prep time: **10 minutes** | Cook time: **25 minutes** | Serves **8 rolls**

- Parchment paper
- 2 cups plus 1 tbsp multigrain flour blend, divided
- 1 tbsp sugar
- 1 (¼-ounce) packet active dry yeast
- 1½ tsp xanthan gum
- 1 tsp sea salt
- ¾ cup water, warmed to 110°F
- 2 tbsp butter, at room temperature, divided
- 2 eggs, at room temperature

1. Line the interior of a 9-inch round cake pan with parchment paper. Set aside.
2. In a large bowl, mix together the flour blend, sugar, yeast, xanthan gum, and salt.
3. Add the water, 1 tbsp of butter, and the eggs. Mix for 30 seconds. Scrape down the sides of the bowl with a spatula. Mix for 3 minutes.
4. Divide the mixture into 8 portions and place them into the cake pan.
5. Place the pan in the warmed oven and let the dough rise for 45 minutes.
6. Remove the pan from the oven. Preheat the oven to 375°F.
7. Melt the remaining 1 tbsp of butter, and brush it on the top of the buns. Bake for 25 minutes, until the tops are golden brown.

CHAPTER 5

HOMEMADE SLIDER BUNS

Prep time: **3 ½ hours** | Cook time: **10 minutes** | Makes **2 lb loaf**

- 1¼ cup milk
- 1 egg
- ¼ cup white sugar
- 2 tbsp butter
- ¾ tsp salt
- 3¾ cups all-purpose flour
- 1 package active dry yeast
- flour (for surface)

1. Add all to the pan of your bread maker.
2. Select the dough cycle in the bread machine.
3. After the dough cycle is finished, lay out the dough to about a 1-inch thickness on a floured surface.
4. A biscuit cutter or a tiny glass cut out 18 buns and set them on a prepared baking sheet.
5. Allow one hour for the buns to rise or until they have doubled in size.
6. Bake for 10 minutes at 350°F (180°C).
7. Brush the melted butter on the tops of the baked buns before serving.

ROSEMARY GARLIC DINNER ROLLS

Prep time: **20 minutes** | Cook time: **15-20 minutes** | Serves **6**

- 1 egg, beaten
- ⅓ cup ground flax seed
- 1 cup mozzarella cheese, shredded
- ½ tsp freshly rosemary, minced
- 1 ounce cream cheese
- ½ tsp baking powder
- 1 cup almond flour

For the Topping:

- ½ tsp rosemary, minced
- Pinch of sea salt
- 1 tbsp butter
- 1 tsp garlic, minced

1. Add all ingredients to the Bread Machine.
2. Select Dough setting. When the time is over, transfer the dough to the floured surface. Shape it into a ball.
3. Roll dough into a log. Slice dough into at least 6 slices. Transfer slices to a greased baking sheet.
4. Melt butter and add garlic along with rosemary; brush half of the mixture on top of biscuits.
5. Bake in a preheated oven at 400 F, for 12-15 minutes.
6. Brush remaining mixture of garlic butter over biscuits with a sprinkle of pinch of salt.

CHAPTER 6: GLUTEN-FREE BREADS

CHAPTER 6

GLUTEN-FREE CINNAMON RAISIN BREAD

Prep time: 5 minutes | Cook time: 15 minutes | Serves 4

- ¾ cup almond milk
- 2 tbsp flax meal
- 6 tbsp warm water
- 1 ½ tsp apple cider vinegar
- 2 tbsp butter
- 1 ½ tbsp honey
- 1 ⅔ cups brown rice flour
- ¼ cup corn starch
- 2 tbsp potato starch
- 1 ½ tsp xanthan gum
- 1 tbsp cinnamon
- ½ tsp salt
- 1 tsp active dry yeast
- ½ cup raisins

1. Mix together flax and water and let stand for 5 minutes.
2. Combine dry ingredients in a separate bowl, except for yeast.
3. Add wet ingredients to the bread machine.
4. Add the dry mixture on top and make a well in the middle of the dry mixture.
5. Add the yeast to the well.
6. Set to Gluten Free, light crust color, and press Start. After first kneading and rise cycle, add raisins.
7. Remove to a cooling rack when baked and let cool for 15 minutes before slicing.

GLUTEN-FREE SORGHUM BREAD

Prep time: 2 ½ hours | Cook time: 10 minutes | Makes 1 ½ lb loaf

- 1½ cups sorghum flour
- 3 tbsp sugar
- 1 cup tapioca starch
- ½ tsp salt
- ½ cup brown or white sweet rice flour
- 1 tsp xanthan gum
- 1 tsp guar gum
- 2¼ tsp instant yeast
- 3 eggs (room temperature, lightly beaten)
- ¼ cup oil
- 1½ tsp vinegar
- ¾ to 1 cup milk warm

1. Except for the yeast, combine the dry in a mixing dish.
2. Place the liquid in the bread maker pan first, followed by the dry.
3. In the center of all the dry, make a well with a finger or a spoon and add the yeast.
4. Set the bread machine setting to the basic bread cycle with a light crust color and hit the Start button.
5. When the bake cycle ends, the bread is ready.
6. Take it out.
7. Before serving, let it cool set it on a wire rack to cool.

GLUTEN-FREE WHITE BREAD

Prep time: 5 minutes | Cook time: 3 hours | Serves 14

- 2 eggs
- 1⅓ cups milk
- 6 tbsp oil
- 1 tsp vinegar
- 3⅝ cups white bread flour
- 1 tsp salt
- 2 tbsp sugar
- 2 tsp dove farm quick yeast

1. Add each ingredient to the bread machine in the order and at the temperature recommended by your bread machine manufacturer.
2. Close the lid and start the machine on the gluten free bread program, if available. Alternatively use the basic or rapid setting with a dark crust option.
3. When the bread machine has finished baking, remove the bread and put it on a cooling rack.

GLUTEN-FREE BREADS

GLUTEN-FREE POTATO BREAD

Prep time: **5 minutes** | Cook time: **3 hours** | Serves **12**

- 1 medium russet potato, baked, or mashed leftovers
- 2 packets gluten-free quick yeast
- 3 tbsp honey
- ¾ cup warm almond milk
- 2 eggs, 1 egg white
- 3 ⅔ cups almond flour
- ¾ cup tapioca flour
- 1 tsp sea salt
- 1 tsp dried chives
- 1 tbsp apple cider vinegar
- ¼ cup olive oil

1. Combine all of the dry ingredients, except the yeast, in a large mixing bowl; set aside.
2. Whisk together the milk, eggs, oil, apple cider, and honey in a separate mixing bowl.
3. Pour the wet ingredients into the bread maker.
4. Add the dry ingredients on top of the wet ingredients.
5. Create a well in the dry ingredients and add the yeast.
6. Set to Gluten-Free bread setting, light crust color, and press Start.
7. Allow to cool completely before slicing.

GLUTEN-FREE MOCK LIGHT RYE

Prep time: **3 hours 40 minutes** | Cook time: **5 minutes** | Serves **6-8**

- 1 ¼ cups water
- 3 tbsp dark molasses
- 1 tsp apple cider or rice vinegar
- ¼ cup vegetable or canola oil
- 3 large eggs, broken into a measuring cup to equal ¾ cup (add water if needed)
- 2 ¼ cups white rice flour
- 1 cup brown rice flour
- 1 cup nonfat dry milk
- ¼ cup dark brown sugar
- 1 tbsp xanthan gum
- 1 tbsp plus 1 tsp caraway seeds
- grated zest of 1 large orange or 2 tsp dried orange peel
- 1 ½ tsp salt
- 2 ¾ tsp bread machine yeast

1. Place all the in the pan according to the order in the manufacturer's instructions. Set crust on dark and
2. program for the Non-Gluten or Quick Yeast Bread cycle; press Start.
3. When the baking cycle ends, immediately remove the pan from the machine and place it on a rack. Let cool for 10 minutes before removing the loaf from the pan. Let the loaf cool to room temperature before slicing.

GLUTEN-FREE PEASANT BREAD

Prep time: **3 hours 40 minutes** | Cook time: **5 minutes** | Serves **6-8**

- 1 ½ tbsp of vegetable oil
- 2 tsp of xanthan gum
- 1 ½ cups of warm water
- 1 tsp of cider vinegar
- 2 cups of gluten-free baking flour
- 1 tbsp of active dry yeast
- 1 tsp of salt
- 2 whole eggs
- 1 tbsp of white sugar

1. Place all in the container of the bread machine in the suggested order by the manufacturer.
2. Select the basic cycle. Light crust. Press the start button.
3. Enjoy fresh bread.

CHAPTER 6

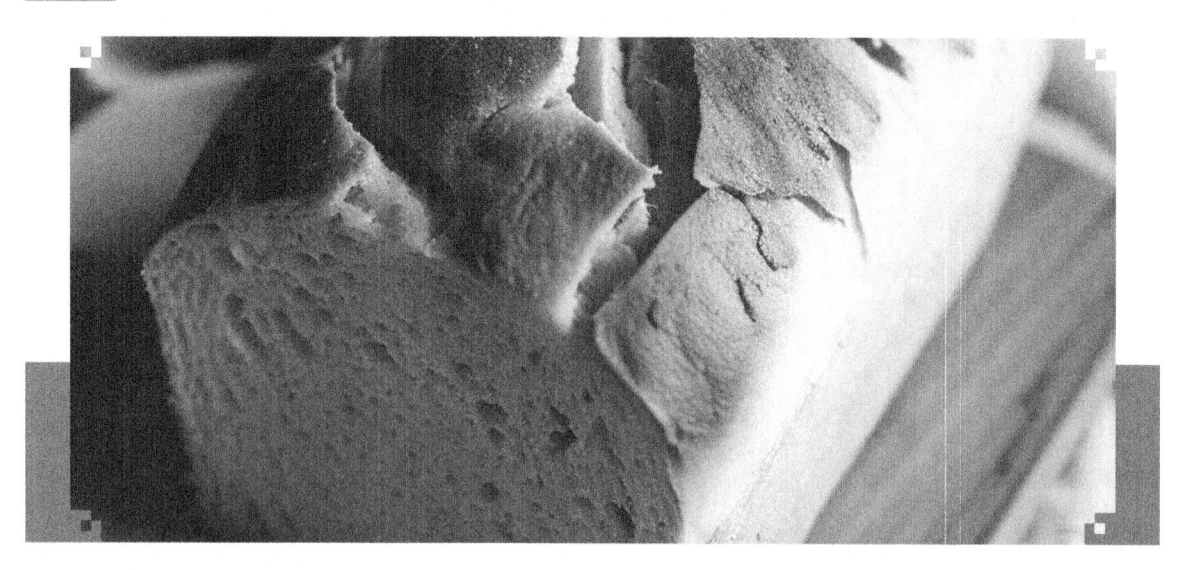

GLUTEN-FREE BUTTERMILK WHITE BREAD

Prep time: 10 minutes | **Cook time:** 20 minutes | Serves 4

- 1 cup buttermilk
- ½ cup water
- 1 tsp apple cider vinegar or rice vinegar
- 4 tbsp butter or margarine, cut into pieces
- 4 large egg whites, beaten until foamy
- 1 cup white rice flour
- 1 cup brown rice flour
- ¾ cup potato starch flour
- ¼ cup tapioca flour
- 3 tbsp light or dark brown sugar
- 1 tbsp plus ½ tsp xanthan gum
- 1½ tsp salt
- 1 tbsp plus 1 tsp SAF yeast or 1 tbsp plus ½ tsp machine yeast

1. Place all the ingredients in the pan according to the order in the manufacturer's instructions. Set crust on medium and program for the Non-Gluten or Quick Yeast Bread cycle; press Start. (This recipe is not suitable for use with the Delay Timer.)
2. When the baking cycle ends, immediately remove the pan from the machine and place it on a rack. Let cool for 10 minutes before removing the loaf from the pan. Let the loaf cool to room temperature before slicing.

GLUTEN-FREE POTATO AND CHIVE BREAD

Prep time: 3 hours | **Cook time:** 10 minutes | Makes 2 lb loaf

- 1¼ cups warm water
- 3 large eggs
- 3 tbsp vegetable oil
- ¾ cup cottage cheese
- 1 tsp cider vinegar
- ½ cup cornstarch
- ½ cup instant potato buds
- ½ cup potato starch
- ½ cup dry skim milk powder
- ½ cup tapioca flour
- ¼ cup snipped fresh chives
- ¼ cup sugar
- 2 cups white rice flour
- 1½ tsp salt
- 2¼ tsp bread machine yeast

1. In the order specified, pour the into the bread pan.
2. Close the cover and secure the bread pan in the baking chamber.
3. Connect to a wall outlet.
4. Choose GLUTEN-FREE.
5. START/STOP by pressing the START/STOP button.
6. When the bread is done, the entire signal will sound.
7. Remove the bread pan from the baking chamber with potholders and carefully remove the bread from the pan. (If the kneading paddle is still in the bread, remove it once it has cooled.)
8. Allow bread to cool on a wire rack for at least 20 minutes before serving.

GLUTEN-FREE BREADS

GLUTEN-FREE CRUSTY BOULE BREAD

Prep time: 3 ½ hours | Cook time: 10 minutes | Makes 1.5 lb loaf

- 3 ¼ cups gluten-free flour mix
- 1 tbsp active dry yeast
- 1 ½ tsp kosher salt
- 1 tbsp guar gum
- 1 ⅓ cups warm water
- 2 large eggs, room temperature
- 2 tbsp, plus 2 tsp olive oil
- 1 tbsp honey

1. Set aside in a large mixing bowl all of the dry, except the yeast.
2. A separate mixing bowl is used to combine the water, eggs, oil, and honey.
3. In a bread machine, combine the wet.
4. On top of the wet components, add the dry.
5. Toss the yeast into a well in the center of the dry.
6. Press Start and select the Gluten-Free option.
7. Pull the baked bread from the oven and set it aside to cool.
8. Hollow out the center, fill with soup or dip, and slice to serve to make a boule.

GLUTEN-FREE OAT & HONEY BREAD

Prep time: 5 minutes | Cook time: 3 hours | Serves 12

- 1 ¼ cups warm water
- 3 tbsp honey
- 2 eggs
- 3 tbsp butter, melted
- 1 ¼ cups gluten-free oats
- 1 ¼ cups brown rice flour
- ½ cup potato starch
- 2 tsp xanthan gum
- 1 ½ tsp sugar
- ¾ tsp salt
- 1 ½ tbsp active dry yeast

1. Add ingredients in the order listed above, except for yeast.
2. Make a well in the center of the dry ingredients and add the yeast.
3. Select Gluten-Free cycle, light crust color, and press Start.
4. Remove bread and allow the bread to cool on its side on a cooling rack for 20 minutes before slicing to serve.

SEEDED GLUTEN-FREE LOAF

Prep time: 5 minutes | Cook time: 15 minutes | Serves 16

- 7 eggs
- 1 cup almond flour
- ½ cup butter
- 2 tbsp. olive oil
- 2 tbsp. chia seeds
- 2 tbsp. sesame seeds
- 1 tsp baking soda
- ½ tsp xanthan gum
- ¼ tsp salt

1. Add eggs and butter to the bread machine pan.
2. Top with all other ingredients.
3. Set bread machine to the gluten-free setting.
4. Once done remove from bread machine and transfer to a cooling rack.
5. This bread can be stored in the fridge for up to 5 days or 3 weeks in the freezer.

CHAPTER 6

GRAIN-FREE CHIA BREAD

Prep time: 5 minutes | Cook time: **3 hours** | Serves **12**

- 1 cup warm water
- 3 large organic eggs, room temperature
- ¼ cup olive oil
- 1 tbsp apple cider vinegar
- 1 cup gluten-free chia seeds, ground to flour
- 1 cup almond meal flour
- ½ cup potato starch
- ¼ cup coconut flour
- ¾ cup millet flour
- 1 tbsp xanthan gum
- 1 ½ tsp salt
- 2 tbsp sugar
- 3 tbsp nonfat dry milk
- 6 tsp instant yeast

1. Whisk wet ingredients together and add to the bread maker pan.
2. Whisk dry ingredients, except yeast, together and add on top of wet ingredients.
3. Make a well in the dry ingredients and add yeast.
4. Select Whole Wheat cycle, light crust color, and press Start.
5. Allow to cool completely before serving.

GLUTEN-FREE RICOTTA POTATO BREAD

Prep time: 3 hours 40 minutes | Cook time: **5 minutes** | Serves **6-8**

- 1 ⅓ cups of water
- ¾ cup ricotta cheese
- 1 tsp apple cider vinegar or rice vinegar
- 3 tbsp vegetable or canola oil
- 3 large eggs, broken into a measuring cup to equal ¾ cup (add water if needed)
- 2 ¼ cups white rice flour
- ½ cup instant potato flakes
- ⅓ cup potato starch flour
- ⅓ cup tapioca flour
- ½ cup dry buttermilk powder or nonfat dry milk
- 3 tbsp sugar or powdered fructose
- 2 tsp xanthan gum
- 1 ½ tsp salt
- ¾ tsp baking soda
- 2 ¾ tsp bread machine yeast

1. Place all the in the pan according to the order in the manufacturer's instructions. Set crust on medium and program for the Non-Gluten or Quick Yeast Bread cycle; press Start
2. When the baking cycle ends, immediately remove the pan from the machine and place it on a rack. Let cool for 10 minutes before removing the loaf from the pan. Let the loaf cool to room temperature before slicing.

GLUTEN-FREE CHICKPEA RICE AND TAPIOCA FLOUR BREAD

Prep time: 2 ½ hours | Cook time: **10 minutes** | Makes **1 ½ lb loaf**

- 1 ¼ cups water
- 1 tsp apple cider vinegar/rice vinegar
- 3 tbsp maple syrup
- 3 tbsp olive oil
- 3 large eggs
- 1 cup chickpea flour
- 1 cup brown rice flour
- ½ cup cornstarch
- ½ cup tapioca flour
- ½ cup nonfat dry milk
- 2 tbsp light brown sugar
- 1 tbsp plus 1 tsp xanthan gum
- 1 ½ tsp salt
- 2 ¾ tsp bread machine yeast

1. Place all of the in the pan in the sequence specified by the maker.
2. Set the crust too dark and click Start on the Non-Gluten or Quick Yeast Bread cycle.
3. (The Delay Timer is not compatible with this recipe.)
4. Remove the pan from the machine and place it on a rack as soon as the baking cycle is through.
5. Allow for a 10-minute cooling period before removing the loaf from the pan.
6. Before slicing, allow the bread to cool to room temperature.

CHAPTER 7: SPICE, NUT & HERB BREADS

CHAPTER 7

SUNFLOWER BREAD

Prep time: **5 minutes** | Cook time: **10 minutes** | Serves **4**

- 12 slice bread (1½ pounds)
- 1 cup water, at 80°F to 90°F
- 1 egg, at room temperature
- 3 tbsp melted butter, cooled
- 3 tbsp skim milk powder
- 1½ tbsp honey
- 1½ tsp salt
- ¾ cup raw sunflower seeds
- 3 cups white bread flour
- 1 tsp bread machine or instant yeast

1. Preparing the Ingredients.
2. Choose the size of loaf of your preference and then measure the ingredients.
3. Add all of the ingredients mentioned previously in the list.
4. Close the lid after placing the pan in the bread machine.
5. Select the Bake cycle
6. Turn on the bread machine. Select the White/Basic setting, select the loaf size, and the crust color. Press start.
7. When the cycle is finished, carefully remove the pan from the bread maker and let it rest.
8. Remove the bread from the pan, put in a wire rack to Cool about 5 minutes. Slice.

RAISIN SEED BREAD

Prep time: **5 minutes** | Cook time: **10 minutes** | Serves **4**

- 12 slice bread (1½ pounds)
- 1 cup plus 2 tbsp milk, at 80°F to 90°F
- 1½ tbsp melted butter, cooled
- 1½ tbsp honey
- ¾ tsp salt
- 3 tbsp flaxseed
- 3 tbsp sesame seeds
- 1¼ cups whole-wheat flour
- 1¾ cups white bread flour
- 1¾ tsp bread machine or instant yeast
- ⅓ cup raisins

1. Preparing the Ingredients.
2. Choose the size of loaf of your preference and then measure the ingredients.
3. Add all of the ingredients mentioned previously in the list except the raisins.
4. Close the lid after placing the pan in the bread machine.
5. Select the Bake cycle
6. Program the machine for Basic/White bread, select light or medium crust, and press Start.
7. Add the raisins when the bread machine signals, or place the raisins in the raisin/nut hopper and let the machine add them.
8. When the cycle is finished, carefully remove the pan from the bread maker and let it rest.
9. Remove the bread from the pan, put in a wire rack to Cool about 5 minutes. Slice.

CUMIN TOSSED FANCY BREAD

Prep time: **3 ½ hours** | Cook time: **10 minutes** | Makes **2 lb loaf**

- 5 ⅓ cups wheat flour
- 1½ tsp salt
- 1½ tbsp sugar
- 1 tbsp dry yeast
- 1¾ cups water
- 2 tbsp cumin
- 3 tbsp sunflower oil

1. Fill the bread machine bucket halfway with warm water.
2. Combine the salt, sugar, and sunflower oil in a mixing bowl.
3. Sift in the wheat flour and stir in the yeast.
4. Set your bread machine's program to French Bread and the rust type to Medium.
5. Add cumin when the maker beeps.
6. Wait till the cycle is finished.
7. When the loaf is done, pull it from the bucket and set it aside to cool for 5 minutes.
8. To remove the bread, gently shake the bucket.

SPICE, NUT & HERB BREADS

FRAGRANT HERB BREAD

Prep time: **5 minutes** | Cook time: **10 minutes** | Serves **4**

- 12 slices bread (1½ pounds)
- 1⅛ cups water, at 80°F to 90°F
- 1½ tbsp melted butter, cooled
- 1½ tbsp sugar
- 1 tsp salt
- 3 tbsp skim milk powder
- 1 tsp dried thyme
- 1 tsp dried chives
- 1 tsp dried oregano
- 3 cups white bread flour
- 1¼ tsp bread machine or instant yeast

1. Preparing the Ingredients.
2. Choose the size of loaf of your preference and then measure the ingredients.
3. Add all of the ingredients mentioned previously in the list. Close the lid after placing the pan in the bread machine.
4. Select the Bake cycle
5. Turn on the bread machine. Select the White/Basic setting, select the loaf size, and the crust color. Press start.
6. When the cycle is finished, carefully remove the pan from the bread maker and let it rest.
7. Remove the bread from the pan, put in a wire rack to Cool about 10 minutes. Slice.

PUMPKIN COCONUT ALMOND BREAD

Prep time: **5 minutes** | Cook time: **5 minutes** | Serves **12**

- ⅓ cup vegetable oil
- 3 large eggs
- 1 ½ cups canned pumpkin puree
- 1 cup sugar
- 1 ½ tsp baking powder
- ½ tsp baking soda
- ¼ tsp salt
- 1 tbsp allspice
- 3 cups all-purpose flour
- ½ cup coconut flakes, plus a small handful for the topping
- ⅔ cup slivered almonds, plus a tbspful for the topping
- Non-stick cooking spray

1. Preparing the Ingredients
2. Spray bread maker pan with non-stick cooking spray. Mix oil, eggs, and pumpkin in a large mixing bowl.
3. Mix remaining ingredients together in a separate mixing bowl. Add wet ingredients to bread maker pan, and dry ingredients on top.
4. Select the Bake cycle
5. Select Dough cycle and press Start. Open lid and sprinkle top of bread with reserved coconut and almonds.
6. Set to Rapid for 1 hour 30 minutes and bake. Cool for 10 minutes on a wire rack before serving.

CHIA SESAME BREAD

Prep time: **3 hours 10 minutes** | Cook time: **5 minutes** | Serves **6-8**

- 1 tbsp of organic apple cider vinegar
- ¼ cup of olive oil
- 2 tsp of salt
- ⅔ cup of almond meal flour
- 3 whole eggs mixed
- 1 cup of ground sesame seeds
- ½ cup of gluten-free tapioca flour
- 1 cup of ground chia seeds
- 1 cup of warm water
- ⅓ cup of Gluten-free coconut flour
- 3 tbsp of psyllium husks ground

1. In a bowl, add all dryand sift them together. Take out any large bits.
2. Put all the require din the container of the bread machine in the suggested order by the manufacturer.
3. Select gluten-free, Press the start button and check dough's consistency. It should not be too wet or too dry. Add 1 tbsp of water or flour if it's too dry or too wet.
4. Serve fresh.

CHAPTER 7

FLAXSEED MILK BREAD

Prep time: **10 minutes** | Cook time: **10 minutes** | Serves **4**

- 16 slice bread (2 pounds)
- 1½ cups lukewarm milk
- 2 tbsp unsalted butter, melted
- 2 tbsp honey
- 2 tsp table salt
- 4 cups white bread flour
- ½ cup flaxseed
- 1½ tsp bread machine yeast

1. Measure and add the ingredients to the pan in the order mentioned above. Place the pan in the bread machine and close the lid.
2. Close the lid, Turn on the bread maker. Select the White / Basic setting, then select the dough size, select light or medium crust. Press start to start the cycle.
3. When this is done, and the bread is baked, remove the pan from the machine. Let stand a few minutes.
4. Remove the bread from the pan and leave it on a wire rack to cool for at least 10 minutes. Slice and serve.

DATE AND NUT BREAD

Prep time: **10 minutes** | Cook time: **10 minutes** | Serves **4**

- 1 cup water
- 1 ½ tbsp. oil
- 2 tbsp. honey
- ½ tsp. salt
- ¾ cup rolled oats
- ¾ cup whole wheat flour
- 1 ½ cups bread flour
- 1 ½ tsp. active dry yeast
- ½ cups, pitted and chopped dates
- ½ cup chopped almonds

1. Place everything into the bread pan according to the bread machine recommendation.
2. Select Fruit bread/Basic cycle and press Start. You can add the dates and nuts after the beep or at the very beginning.

CALIFORNIA NUT BREAD

Prep time: **10 minutes** | Cook time: **5 to 7 minutes** | Serves **4**

- 1 cup (4 to 5 ounces) nutmeat pieces
- 1⅔ cups buttermilk
- ½ cup nut oil
- 4 cups bread flour
- 1½ tbsp dark brown sugar
- 1 tbsp plus 1 tsp gluten
- 2 tsp salt
- 1 tbsp SAF yeast or 1 tbsp plus ½ tsp bread machine yeast

1. Preheat the oven to 350°F.
2. Spread the nuts evenly on a baking sheet. Bake until lightly toasted, about 5 to 7 minutes. Remove from the oven and let cool.
3. Place the ingredients, except the nuts, in the pan according to the order in the manufacturer's instructions. Set crust on medium or dark and program for the Basic cycle; press Start. (This recipe is not suitable for use with the Delay Timer.) When the machine beeps or between Knead 1 and Knead 2, add the nuts. Test the dough with your fingers. If it is very firm and dry, maybe even lumpy, add another tbsp of buttermilk to soften it up a bit.
4. When the baking cycle ends, immediately remove the bread from the pan and place it on a rack. Let cool to room temperature before slicing.

SPICE, NUT & HERB BREADS

CUMIN BREAD

Prep time: **3 ½ hours** | Cook time: **10 minutes** | Makes **2 lb Loaf**

- 4 cups bread machine flour
- 1½ tsp kosher salt
- 1½ tbsp sugar
- 1 tbsp bread machine yeast
- 1¾ cups lukewarm water
- 1 tbsp black cumin
- 1 tbsp sunflower oil

1. Place all dry and liquid in the pan and bake according to your bread machine's .
2. Then set the crust type to MEDIUM and the baking program to BASIC.
3. Adjust the amount of flour and liquid in the recipe if the dough is too dense or too wet.
4. Take the pan from the bread machine after the program has finished and set it aside to cool for 5 minutes.
5. Remove the bread from the pan by shaking it.
6. Use a spatula if required.
7. Set the bread aside for an hour after wrapping it in a kitchen towel.
8. You may also cool it on a wire rack.

TURMERIC BREAD

Prep time: **10 minutes** | Cook time: **15 minutes** | Serves **4**

- 1 tsp dried yeast
- 4 cups strong white flour
- 1 tsp turmeric powder
- 2 tsp beetroot powder
- 2 tbsp olive oil
- 1.5 tsp salt
- 1 tsp chili flakes
- 1⅜ water

1. Add each ingredient to the bread machine in the order and at the temperature recommended by your bread machine manufacturer.
2. Close the lid, select the basic bread, medium crust setting on your bread machine and press start.
3. When the bread machine has finished baking, remove the bread and put it on a cooling rack.

CRACKED BLACK PEPPER BREAD

Prep time: **5 minutes** | Cook time: **10 minutes** | Serves **4**

- 12 slice bread (1½ pounds)
- 1⅛ cups water, at 80°F to 90°F
- 1½ tbsp melted butter, cooled
- 1½ tbsp sugar
- 1 tsp salt
- 3 tbsp skim milk powder
- 1½ tbsp minced chives
- ¾ tsp garlic powder
- ¾ tsp freshly cracked black pepper
- 3 cups white bread flour
- 1¼ tsp bread machine or instant yeast

1. Preparing the Ingredients.
2. Choose the size of loaf of your preference and then measure the ingredients.
3. Add all of the ingredients mentioned previously in the list.
4. Close the lid after placing the pan in the bread machine.
5. Select the Bake cycle
6. Turn on the bread machine. Select the White/Basic setting, select the loaf size, and the crust color. Press start.
7. When the cycle is finished, carefully remove the pan from the bread maker and let it rest.
8. Remove the bread from the pan, put in a wire rack to Cool about 10 minutes. Slice.

CHAPTER 7

TOASTED WALNUT BREAD

Prep time: **3 hours 40 minutes** | Cook time: **5 minutes** | Serves **6-8**

- ¾ cup walnut pieces
- 1 cup of water
- 2 large egg whites, lightly beaten
- 1 ½ tbsp butter, cut into pieces
- 3 cups of bread flour
- 2 tbsp sugar
- 2 tbsp nonfat dry milk
- 1 tbsp gluten
- ¾ tsp salt
- 2 tsp bread machine yeast

1. Preheat the oven to 350°F.
2. Spread the walnuts on a baking sheet and place in the center of the oven for 4 minutes to toast lightly. Set aside to cool.
3. Place the ingredients, except the walnuts, in the pan according to the order in the manufacturer's instructions.
4. Set crust on medium and program for the Basic or Fruit and Nut cycle; press Start. When the machine beeps, or between Knead 1 Knead 2, add the walnuts.
5. When the baking cycle ends, immediately remove the pan's bread and place it on a rack. Let cool to room temperature before slicing.

HERBED PESTO BREAD

Prep time: **10 minutes** | Cook time: **15 minutes** | Serves **4**

- 12 slices bread (1½ pounds)
- 1 cup water, at 80°F to 90°F
- 2¼ tbsp melted butter, cooled
- 1½ tsp minced garlic
- ¾ tbsp sugar
- 1 tsp salt
- 3 tbsp chopped fresh parsley
- 1½ tbsp chopped fresh basil
- ⅓ cup grated Parmesan cheese
- 3 cups white bread flour
- 1¼ tsp bread machine or active dry yeast

1. Choose the size of loaf of your preference and then measure the ingredients.
2. Add all of the ingredients mentioned previously in the list.
3. Close the lid after placing the pan in the bread machine.
4. Turn on the bread machine. Select the White/Basic setting, select the loaf size, and the crust color. Press start.
5. When the cycle is finished, carefully remove the pan from the bread maker and let it rest.
6. Remove the bread from the pan, put in a wire rack to Cool about 10 minutes. Slice

CHAPTER 8: VEGETABLE AND FRUIT BREADS

CHAPTER 8

BEETROOT BREAD

Prep time: 5 minutes | Cook time: 10 minutes | Serves 4

- 16 slice bread (2 pounds)
- 1 cup lukewarm water
- 1 cup grated raw beetroot
- 2 tbsp unsalted butter, melted
- 2 tbsp sugar
- 2 tsp table salt
- 4 cups white bread flour
- 1⅔ tsp bread machine yeast

- 12 slice bread (1½ pounds)
- ¾ cups lukewarm water
- ¾ cup grated raw beetroot
- 1½ tbsp unsalted butter, melted
- 1½ tbsp sugar
- 1¼ tsp table salt
- 3 cups white bread flour
- 1¼ tsp bread machine yeast

1. Choose the size of loaf you would like to make and measure your ingredients.
2. Add the ingredients to the bread pan in the order listed above.
3. Place the pan in the bread machine and close the lid.
4. Turn on the bread maker. Select the White/Basic setting, then the loaf size, and finally the crust color. Start the cycle.
5. When the cycle is finished and the bread is baked, carefully remove the pan from the machine. Use a potholder as the handle will be very hot. Let rest for a few minutes.
6. Remove the bread from the pan and allow to cool on a wire rack for at least 10 minutes before slicing.

TOMATO BASIL BREAD

Prep time: 5 minutes | Cook time: 4 hours | Serves 16

- ¾ cup warm water
- ¼ cup fresh basil, minced
- ¼ cup parmesan cheese, grated
- 3 tbsp tomato paste
- 1 tbsp sugar
- 1 tbsp olive oil
- 1 tsp salt
- ¼ tsp crushed red pepper flakes
- 2 ½ cups bread flour
- 1 package active dry yeast
- Flour, for surface

1. Add ingredients, except yeast, to bread maker pan in above listed order.
2. Make a well in the flour; pour the yeast into the hole.
3. Select Dough cycle and press Start.
4. Turn finished dough out onto a floured surface and knead until smooth and elastic, about 3 to 5 minutes.
5. Place in a greased bowl, turning once to grease top. Cover and let rise in a warm place until doubled, about 1 hour.
6. Punch dough down and knead for 1 minute.
7. Shape into a round loaf. Place on a greased baking sheet. Cover and let rise until doubled, about 1 hour.
8. With a sharp knife, cut a large "X" in top of loaf. Bake at 375°F for 35-40 minutes or until golden brown.
9. Remove from pan and cool on a cooling rack before serving.

SAGE AND ONION LOAF

Prep time: 3 hours 10 minutes | Cook time: 5 minutes | Serves 6

- ⅓ cup of butter
- 1 large onion, finely chopped
- 1 tsp Easy bake yeast
- 1 ¾ cups of strong white bread flour
- 1 ¾ cups of strong whole meal flour
- 1 tsp fine sea salt
- ¼ tsp freshly ground black pepper
- 1 ⅔ cups of water
- 2 tbsp chopped fresh sage or 1 tbsp dried

1. Melt the butter in a pan, add the onion and cook gently for about 10 minutes, occasionally stirring, until very soft but not browned. Alternatively, put the butter and onion into a casserole, cover, and microwave on high for 5 minutes, stirring once, until very soft. Leave to cool.
2. Put the remaining into the pan in the correct order for your machine. Add the buttery onion mixture.

VEGETABLE AND FRUIT BREADS

PUMPKIN RAISIN BREAD

Prep time: 5 minutes | Cook time: 1 hour and 30 minutes | Serves 4

- ½ cup all-purpose flour
- ½ cup whole-wheat flour
- ½ cup pumpkin, mashed
- ½ cup raisins
- ¼ cup brown sugar
- 2 tbsp baking powder
- 1 tsp salt
- 1 tsp pumpkin pie spice
- ¼ tsp baking soda
- ¾ cup apple juice
- ¼ cup of vegetable oil
- 3 tbsp aquafaba

1. Place all ingredients in the bread pan in this order: apple juice, pumpkin, oil, aquafaba, flour, sugar, baking powder, baking soda, salt, pumpkin pie spice, and raisins.
2. Select the "Quick" or "Cake" mode of your bread machine.
3. Let the machine finish all cycles.
4. Remove the pan from the machine.
5. After 10 minutes, transfer the bread to a wire rack.
6. Slice the bread only when it has completely cooled down.

PINEAPPLE JUICE BREAD

Prep time: 2 hours | Cook time: 10 minutes | Makes 1 ½ lb loaf

- ¾ cup fresh pineapple juice
- 1 egg
- 2 tbsp vegetable oil
- 2 ½ tbsp honey
- ¾ tsp salt
- 3 cups bread flour
- 2 tbsp dry milk powder
- 2 tsp quick-rising yeast

1. Place all in the bread machine's baking pan in the manufacturer's recommended order.
2. Close the cover on the bread maker and place the baking pan inside.
3. Select the Sweet Bread option, followed by Light Crust.
4. To begin, press the start button.
5. The bread is done when the bake cycle is finished.
6. Remove the baking pan carefully from the machine, and invert the bread loaf onto a wire rack to cool entirely before slicing.
7. Cut the bread loaf into desired-sized slices with a sharp knife and serve.

ZUCCHINI BREAD

Prep time: 5 minutes | Cook time: 10 minutes | Serves 12

- ½ tsp salt
- 1 cup sugar
- 1 tbsp pumpkin pie spice
- 1 tbsp baking powder
- 1 tsp pure vanilla extract
- ⅓ cup milk
- ½ cup vegetable oil
- 2 eggs
- 2 cups bread flour
- 1 ½ tsp active dry yeast or bread machine yeast
- 1 cup shredded zucchini, raw and unpeeled
- 1 cup of chopped walnuts (optional)

1. Preparing the Ingredients
2. Add all of the ingredients for the zucchini bread into the bread maker pan in the order listed above, reserving yeast.
3. Make a well in the center of the dry ingredients and add the yeast.
4. Select the Bake cycle
5. Select Wheat bread cycle, medium crust color, and press Start.
6. Transfer to a cooling rack for 10 to 15 minutes before slicing to serve.

CHAPTER 8

CRANBERRY ORANGE BREAD

Prep time: 2 ½ hours | Cook time: 10 minutes | Makes 1 ½ pound loaf

- 2 tbsp active dry yeast
- 3 cups Light Flour Blend
- 1 cup granulated cane sugar
- 1 tbsp psyllium husk flakes or powder
- 2 tsp baking powder
- 1 tsp kosher or fine sea salt
- 3 large eggs (beaten)
- ½ cup water
- ½ cup orange juice
- ¼ cup vegetable or canola oil
- 2 tsp apple cider vinegar
- 2 cups fresh or frozen cranberries

1. Place the bread pan on the counter with the beater paddle inside.
2. Add the water first in the pan, then the dry except for the yeast.
3. In the center of these , make a well with a spoon and add the yeast.
4. Insert the bread pan into the machine, center it, and lock it in place.
5. Close the lid and choose from the following option: Cycle gluten-free with 1 ½ pound/750 g Loaf size: pick Medium crust, and then hit Start.
6. When the baking is finished, take the bread pan from the machine and place it on a wire cooling rack on its side.
7. Allow for a few minutes in the pan before turning it upside down and sliding the loaf onto the wire rack.
8. Allow the bread to cool before slicing it upside down.

APPLE SPICE BREAD

Prep time: 5 minutes | Cook time: 10 minutes | Serves 4

- 16 slice bread (2 pounds)
- 1⅓ cup milk, at 80°F to 90°F
- 3⅓ tbsp melted butter, cooled
- 2⅔ tbsp sugar
- 2 tsp salt
- 1⅓ tsp ground cinnamon
- Pinch ground cloves
- 4 cups white bread flour
- 2¼ tsp bread machine or active dry yeast
- 1⅓ cups finely diced peeled apple

1. Preparing the Ingredients.
2. Choose the size of loaf of your preference and then measure the ingredients.
3. Add all of the ingredients mentioned previously in the list, except for the apple. Close the lid after placing the pan in the bread machine.
4. Select the Bake cycle
5. Turn on the bread machine. White/Basic or Fruit/Nut (if your machine has this setting) setting, select the loaf size, and the crust color. Press start.
6. When the machine signals to add ingredients, add the apple. When the cycle is finished, carefully remove the pan from the bread maker and let it rest.
7. Remove the bread from the pan, put in a wire rack to cool for at least 10 minutes, and slice.
8. Fit the pan into the bread machine and close the lid. Select the basic white setting, medium crust, and the appropriate size. Press Start.
9. When the program has finished, lift the pan out of the machine, turn the bread out onto a wire rack and leave to cool completely.

VEGETABLE AND FRUIT BREADS

STRAWBERRY SHORTCAKE BREAD

Prep time: **3 hours 10 minutes** | Cook time: **5 minutes** | Serves **6**

- 2 ½ tsp of bread machine yeast
- 1 tsp of vanilla extract
- ¼ cup of warm heavy whipping cream
- 3 cups of bread machine flour
- ¼ cup of warm water
- 1 tbsp of sugar
- 1/8 tsp of baking powder
- 2 cups of fresh strawberries with ¼ cup sugar
- 1 tsp of salt

1. Add water, cream to the pan of the bread maker, mix with yeast and sugar. Let it rest for 15 minutes.
2. Coat the sliced strawberries with ¼ cup of sugar.
3. Add all ingredients, except for strawberries, to the bread machine in the manufacturer's suggested order.
4. Add strawberries to the fruit hopper or add at the signal.
5. Select basic, medium crust. Press the start button.
6. Slice and serve fresh bread.

CINNAMON & DRIED FRUITS BREAD

Prep time: **3 hours** | Cook time: **10 minutes** | Makes **1 lb loaf**

- 2 ¾ cups flour
- ¾ cup water
- 1 ½ cups dried fruits
- 4 tbsp sugar
- 2½ tbsp butter
- 1 tbsp milk powder
- 1 tsp cinnamon
- ½ tsp ground nutmeg
- ¼ tsp vanillin
- ½ cup peanuts powdered sugar (for sprinkling)
- 1 tsp salt
- 1½ bread machine yeast

1. Follow the manufacturer's for adding all to your bread machine (except the peanuts and powdered sugar).
2. Set your bread machine's program to Basic/White Bread and the crust type to Medium.
3. When the bread maker beeps, wet the dough with a little water and sprinkle in the dried fruits.
4. Wait till the cycle is finished.
5. When the loaf is done, take it from the bucket and set it aside to cool for 5 minutes.
6. To remove the bread, gently shake the bucket.
7. Sprinkle with sugar powder.

FETA AND SPINACH BREAD

Prep time: **10 minutes** | Cook time: **10 minutes** | Serves **4**

- 2 cups water
- 1 cup frozen chopped spinach (defrosted and squeezed dry)
- 3 tbsp olive oil
- 4 cups bread flour
- 5 ounces crumbled feta cheese
- 1½ tbsp sugar
- 1 tsp salt
- 2¼ tsp SAF yeast or 2¾ tsp bread machine yeast

1. Place all the ingredients in the pan according to the order in the manufacturer's instructions. Set crust on medium and program for the Basic cycle; press Start. (This recipe is not suitable for use with the Delay Timer.)
2. When the baking cycle ends, immediately remove the bread from the pan and place it on a rack. Let cool to room temperature before slicing.

CHAPTER 8

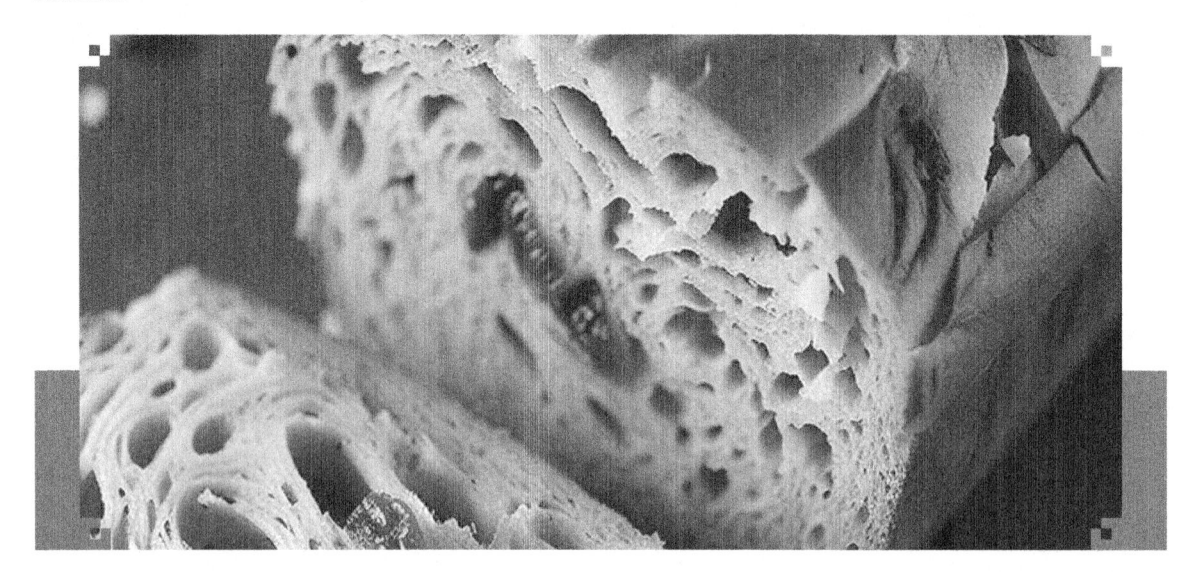

TOMATO ONION BREAD

Prep time: 5 minutes | **Cook time: 1 hour and 30 minutes** | **Serves 12**

- 2 cups all-purpose flour
- 1 cup wholemeal flour
- ½ cup of warm water
- 4¾ ounces milk
- 3 tbsp olive oil
- 2 tbsp sugar
- 1 tsp salt
- 2 tsp dry yeast
- ½ tsp baking powder
- 5 sun-dried tomatoes
- 1 onion
- ¼ tsp black pepper

1. Prepare all the necessary products. Finely chop the onion and sauté in a frying pan. Cut up the sun-dried tomatoes (10 halves).
2. Pour all liquid ingredients into the bowl, then cover with flour and put in the tomatoes and onions. Pour in the yeast and baking powder without touching the liquid.
3. Select the baking mode and start. You can choose the Bread with Additives program, and then the bread maker will knead the dough at low speeds. I chose the usual baking mode the kneading was very active, and the vegetables practically dissolved in the dough. For children who like to find something in the food and carefully remove it from it (for example, pieces of onions), this is an ideal option!
4. Enjoy!

PLUM ORANGE BREAD

Prep time: 5 minutes | **Cook time: 10 minutes** | **Serves 4**

- 12 slice bread (1½ pounds)
- 1⅛ cup water, at 80°F to 90°F
- 2¼ tbsp melted butter, cooled
- 3 tbsp sugar
- ¾ tsp salt
- ¾ tsp orange zest
- ⅓ tsp ground cinnamon
- Pinch ground nutmeg
- 1¾ cups plus 2 tbsp whole-wheat flour
- 1⅛ cups white bread flour
- 1½ tsp bread machine or instant yeast
- 1 cup chopped fresh plums

1. Preparing the Ingredients.
2. Choose the size of loaf of your preference and then measure the ingredients.
3. Add all of the ingredients mentioned previously in the list, except for the plums. Close the lid after placing the pan in the bread machine.
4. Select the Bake cycle
5. Turn on the bread machine. White/Basic or Fruit/Nut (if your machine has this setting) setting, select the loaf size, and the crust color. Press start.
6. When the machine signals to add ingredients, add the plums. When the cycle is finished, carefully remove the pan from the bread maker and let it rest.
7. Remove the bread from the pan, put in a wire rack to cool for at least 10 minutes, and slice.

CHAPTER 9: SWEET & SAVORY BREADS

CHAPTER 9

SWEET POTATO BREAD

Prep time: **10 minutes** | Cook time: **10 minutes** | Serves **6**

- ⅔ cup fat-free milk
- 1 cup pureed sweet potatoes
- ¼ cup sour cream
- 4 cups bread flour
- 1 tbsp plus 1 tsp gluten
- 2 tsp salt
- Grated zest of 1 orange
- 2½ tsp SAF yeast or 1 tbsp bread machine yeast
- 7/8 cup fresh whole cranberries

1. Place the ingredients, except the cranberries, in the pan according to the order in the manufacturer's instructions. Set crust on medium and program for the Basic or Fruit and Nut cycle; press Start. (This recipe is not suitable for use with the Delay Timer.) When the machine beeps, or between Knead 1 and Knead 2, add the cranberries; they will break up some with the action of the blade.
2. When the baking cycle ends, immediately remove the bread from the pan and place it on a rack. Let cool to room temperature before slicing.

PEANUT BUTTER BREAD

Prep time: **1 hour** | Cook time: **10 minutes** | Makes **1,5 lb loaf**

- 1 cup + 1 tbsp water
- ½ cup peanut butter
- 3 cups bread flour
- 3 tbsp brown sugar
- 1 tsp salt
- 2 tsp bread machine yeast

1. Collect the necessary components.
2. In the bread machine, combine the water, salt, bread flour, peanut butter, brown sugar, and bread machine yeast in the sequence indicated by the manufacturer, carefully measuring each ingredient.
3. Choose between the "Sweet" and "Basic/White" cycles.
4. Turn the machine on and select "Medium" or "Light Crust Color." When the bread is done, it should be a dark gold color with a hollow sound when tapped with your fingers.
5. Check the temperature of the bread, which should be around 210 degrees Fahrenheit.
6. Let it cool on a wire rack before serving.

CHOCOLATE MARBLE CAKE

Prep time: **5 minutes** | Cook time: **3 hours 45 minutes** | Serves **12 to 16**

- 1 ½ cups water
- 1 ½ tsp vanilla extract
- 1 ½ tsp salt
- 3 ½ cups bread flour
- 1 ½ tsp instant yeast
- 1 cup semi-sweet chocolate chips

1. Set the chocolate chips aside and add the other ingredients to the pan of your bread maker.
2. Program the machine for Sweet bread and press Start.
3. Check the dough after 10 to 15 minutes of kneading; you should have a smooth ball, soft but not sticky.
4. Add the chocolate chips about 3 minutes before the end of the second kneading cycle.
5. Once baked, remove with a rubber spatula and allow to cool on a rack before serving.

SWEET & SAVORY BREADS

BLUE CHEESE ONION BREAD

Prep time: **5 minutes** | Cook time: **10 minutes** | Serves **4**

- 12 slice bread (1½ pounds)
- 1¼ cup water, at 80°F to 90°F
- 1 egg, at room temperature
- 1 tbsp melted butter, cooled
- ¼ cup powdered skim milk
- 1 tbsp sugar
- ¾ tsp salt
- ½ cup (2 ounces) crumbled blue cheese
- 1 tbsp dried onion flakes
- 3 cups white bread flour
- ¼ cup instant mashed potato flakes
- 1 tsp bread machine or active dry yeast

1. Preparing the Ingredients.
2. Choose the size of loaf of your preference and then measure the ingredients.
3. Add all of the ingredients mentioned previously in the list.
4. Close the lid after placing the pan in the bread machine.
5. Select the Bake cycle
6. Turn on the bread machine. Select the Quick/Rapid setting, select the loaf size, and the crust color. Press start.
7. When the cycle is finished, carefully remove the pan from the bread maker and let it rest.
8. Remove the bread from the pan, put in a wire rack to Cool about 10 minutes. Slice.

JALAPEÑO CORN BREAD

Prep time: **5 minutes** | Cook time: **10 minutes** | Serves **4**

- 12 to 16 slices bread (1½ to 2 pounds)
- 1 cup buttermilk, at 80°F to 90°F
- ¼ cup melted butter, cooled
- 2 eggs, at room temperature
- 1 jalapeño pepper, chopped
- 1⅓ cups all-purpose flour
- 1 cup cornmeal
- ½ cup (2 ounces) shredded Cheddar cheese
- ¼ cup sugar
- 1 tbsp baking powder
- ½ tsp salt

1. Preparing the Ingredients.
2. Choose the size of loaf of your preference and then measure the ingredients.
3. Add all of the ingredients mentioned previously in the list.
4. Close the lid after placing the pan in the bread machine.
5. Select the Bake cycle
6. Turn on the bread machine. Select the Quick/Rapid setting, select the loaf size, and the crust color. Press start.
7. When the cycle is finished, carefully remove the pan from the bread maker and let it rest.
8. Remove the bread from the pan, put in a wire rack to Cool about 5 minutes. Slice.

HONEY BREAD

Prep time: **5 minutes** | Cook time: **2 hours** | Serves **16**

- 1 cup plus 1 tbsp milk
- 3 tbsp honey
- 3 tbsp butter, melted
- 3 cups bread flour
- 1½ tsp salt
- 2 tsp active dry yeast

1. Place all ingredients in the baking pan of bread machine in the order recommended by manufacturer.
2. Place the baking pan in bread machine and close with lid.
3. Select "White Bread" setting and then "Medium Crust".
4. Press start button.
5. Carefully, remove the baking pan from machine and then invert the bread loaf onto a wire rack to cool completely before slicing.
6. With a sharp knife, cut bread loaf into desired-sized slices and serve.

CHAPTER 9

SAMPLER HAWAIIAN SWEET LOAF

Prep time: **10 minutes** | Cook time: **20 minutes** | Serves **4**

- 1 cup evaporated milk
- One 8-ounce can crushed pineapple in its own juice
- ¼ cup pineapple juice reserved from draining the canned pineapple
- 1 tbsp vegetable or nut oil
- 2 cups bread flour
- ⅓ cup flaked coconut
- 1½ tbsp light brown sugar
- 2 tsp gluten
- 1 tsp salt
- ½ tsp ground ginger
- 1½ tsp SAF yeast or 2 tsp bread machine yeast
- ¼ cup coarsely chopped macadamia nuts, rinsed and dried on a paper towel if salted

1. Place all the ingredients in the pan according to the order in the manufacturer's instructions. Set crust on dark and program for the Whole Wheat cycle; press Start. (This recipe is not suitable for use with the Delay Timer.)
2. When the baking cycle ends, immediately remove the bread from the pan and place it on a rack. Let cool to room temperature before slicing.

ROASTED GARLIC AND DRY JACK BREAD

Prep time: **3 hours 10 minutes** | Cook time: **5 minutes** | Serves **6-8**

- 3 to 4 ounces (1 to 2 heads) garlic
- 1 ¼ cups water
- 3 cups of bread flour
- ½ cup grated dry jack cheese
- 2 tsp gluten
- 1 ¾ tsp salt
- 1 tbsp bread machine yeast

1. Preheat the oven to 350°F.
2. Place the garlic in a small baking dish and bake until soft when touched with your finger, 40 to 45 minutes. Remove from the oven and let cool to room temperature.
3. Cut the head of roasted garlic in half horizontally. Place all the in the pan according to the order in the manufacturer's instructions, squeezing out the cloves of garlic and dropping them into the pan along with the water.
4. Set crust on medium and program for the Basic or French Bread cycle; press Start.
5. When the baking cycle ends, immediately remove the pan's bread and place it on a rack. Let cool to room temperature before slicing.

CHERRY CHOCOLATE BREAD

Prep time: **3 ½ hours** | Cook time: **10 minutes** | Makes **2 lb loaf**

- 1⅓ cups milk
- 1 large egg
- ¾ tsp vanilla extract
- ¾ tsp almond extract
- 4 tbsp unsalted butter
- 3¾ cups bread flour
- ½ cup unsweetened Dutch-process cocoa powder
- ⅓ cup light brown sugar
- 1 tbsp + 1 tsp gluten
- 1½ tsp salt
- 1 tbsp active dry yeast
- 1 cup snipped glacéed tart dried cherries

1. In the sequence specified in the manufacturer's directions, place all in the pan, except the cherries.
2. Set the crust to medium and begin the Basic or Sweet Bread cycle by pressing the Start button.
3. (The Delay Timer is not compatible with this recipe.) Add the cherries when the machine whistles or between Knead 1 and Knead 2.
4. Take out the bread from the pan and place it on a rack when the baking cycle is finished.
5. Before slicing, allow it cool to room temperature.

SWEET & SAVORY BREADS

DUTCH SUGAR LOAF

Prep time: **10 minutes** | Cook time: **20 minutes** | Serves **4**

- ¾ cup sugar cubes
- 2 tsp ground cinnamon
- Small pinch of ground cloves
- 2 cups fat-free milk
- 2 tbsp unsalted butter or margarine, cut into pieces
- 4 cups bread flour
- 1 tbsp plus 1 tsp gluten
- 1¾ tsp salt
- 2½ tsp SAF yeast or 1 tbsp bread machine yeast

1. Place the sugar cubes in a heavy clear plastic freezer bag and, using the smooth side of a meat hammer, crack the cubes. Don't crush them; you want the chunks to be no smaller than quarter cubes, if possible. Add the spices to the bag and toss to coat. Set aside.
2. Place the ingredients, except the spice-coated sugar cubes, in the pan according to the order in the manufacturer's instructions. Set crust on medium, and program for the Sweet Bread cycle; press Start. (This recipe is not suitable for use with the Delay Timer.) Five minutes into the kneading segment, press Pause and sprinkle in half of the sugar cube mixture. Press Start to resume the cycle. Three minutes later, press Pause and add the rest of the sugar cube mixture. Press Start to resume the cycle.
3. When the baking cycle ends, immediately remove the bread from the pan and place it on a rack. Let cool to room temperature before slicing, or sugar syrup will ooze out.

CHEESE, HAM, AND CHILE STRATA

Prep time: **10 minutes** | Cook time: **50 minutes** | Serves **8**

- 3 cups (10 to 12 ounces) coarsely chopped cooked ham, such as honey-baked
- 2 large cans (7 ounces each) diced, roasted green chiles
- 1 pound mild cheddar cheese, shredded (about 4 cups)
- 5 cups milk
- 10 large eggs
- 1½ tsp dried basil or oregano
- Fresh-ground black pepper to taste

1. Arrange a quarter of the bread slices, slightly overlapping, in the bottom of a shallow 4-quart casserole. Top with a third of the ham; then a layer of the green chiles and then 1 cup of the cheese. Arrange another layer of bread over this, barely covering the filling. Continue to layer the ham, chiles, cheese, and bread to make a total of 4 layers of bread and 3 layers of filling, finishing with the bread slices on top. (You will have 1 cup of cheese left for topping.)
2. Whisk together the milk, eggs, and seasonings in a large bowl. Slowly pour over the bread. Sprinkle the top with the last cup of the cheese, cover tightly, and refrigerate at least 2 hours to overnight.
3. When ready to bake, preheat the oven to 325°F.
4. Bake uncovered for 50 minutes to 1 hour, or until the center is puffed and golden; a knife inserted into the center will come out clean. Let stand for 10 minutes before serving hot.

CHAPTER 9

CHOCOLATE OATMEAL BANANA BREAD

Prep time: **5 minutes** | Cook time: **10 minutes** | Serves **4**

- 12 to 16 slice bread (1½ to 2 pounds)
- 3 bananas, mashed
- 2 eggs, at room temperature
- ¾ cup packed light brown sugar
- ½ cup (1 stick) butter, at room temperature
- ½ cup sour cream, at room temperature
- ¼ cup sugar
- 1½ tsp pure vanilla extract
- 1 cup all-purpose flour
- ½ cup quick oats
- 2 tbsp unsweetened cocoa powder
- 1 tsp baking soda

1. Preparing the Ingredients.
2. Place the banana, eggs, brown sugar, butter, sour cream, sugar, and vanilla in your bread machine.
3. Program the machine for Quick/Rapid bread and press Start.
4. While the wet ingredients are mixing, stir together the flour, oats, cocoa powder, and baking soda in a small bowl.
5. Select the Bake cycle
6. After the first fast mixing is done and the machine signals, add the dry ingredients.
7. When the loaf is done, remove the bucket from the machine.
8. Let the loaf cool for 5 minutes.
9. Gently shake the bucket to remove the loaf, and turn it out onto a rack to cool.

MOZZARELLA CHEESE AND SALAMI LOAF

Prep time: **5 minutes** | Cook time: **10 minutes**| Serves **4**

- ¾ cup water, set at 80 °F
- ⅓ cup mozzarella cheese, shredded
- 4 tsp sugar
- ⅔ tsp salt
- ⅔ tsp dried basil
- Pinch of garlic powder
- 2 cups + 2 tbsp white bread flour
- 1 tsp instant yeast
- ½ cup hot salami, finely diced

1. Add the listed ingredients to your bread machine (except salami), following the manufactures instructions.
2. Set the bread machine's program to Basic/White Bread and the crust type to light. Press Start.
3. Let the bread machine work and wait until it beeps. This your indication to add the remaining ingredients at this point, add the salami.
4. Wait until the remaining bake cycle completes.
5. Once the loaf is done, take the bucket out from the bread machine and let it rest for 5 minutes.
6. Gently shake the bucket and remove the loaf, transfer the loaf to a cooling rack and slice.
7. Serve and enjoy!

CHAPTER 10: NO-YEAST BREADS

CHAPTER 10

BOURBON NUT QUICK BREAD

Prep time: 2 ½ hours | Cook time: 10 minutes | Makes 2 lb loaf

- 2 large eggs
- 2¼ cups unbleached all-purpose flour
- ¼ cup nut oil/vegetable oil
- 1½ tsp almond extract
- 1½ cups sour cream
- ½ cup bourbon
- ½ tsp salt
- ½ tsp baking soda
- 1 cup light brown sugar
- 2½ tsp baking powder
- 1½ tsp ground nutmeg
- 1 tsp instant espresso powder
- 1¼ cups coarsely chopped pecans/walnuts

1. In the pan, layer the in the sequence specified in the manufacturer's directions.
2. Set the crust too dark if your machine has that option, and set up the machine for the Quick Bread/Cake cycle; push Start.
3. When the bread shrinks slightly from the pan's sides, the sides are dark brown, and the top is firm to a mild pressure when touched with your finger, it's done.
4. Allow 10 minutes for the bread to cool in the pan before flipping it out, right side up, to cool entirely on a rack.
5. Before serving, wrap firmly in plastic wrap and chill for at least 3 days.

GOLDEN CORN BREAD

Prep time: 2 hours | Cook time: 10 minutes | Makes 1 lb loaf

- 2 cups all-purpose flour
- 1 cup buttermilk
- 1 tbsp baking powder
- 2 eggs
- 1 cup cornmeal
- ¼ cup sugar
- 1 tsp salt
- ¼ cup melted butter

1. Follow the manufacturer's recommendations for adding buttermilk, butter, and eggs to your bread machine.
2. Press START after programming the machine for Quick/Rapid Bread mode.
3. While the wet are being combined in the machine, combine flour, cornmeal, sugar, baking powder, and salt in a small bowl.
4. When the machine indicates that the first rapid mix is complete, add the dry .
5. Wait until the entire cycle is finished.
6. Remove the bucket from the oven after the loaf is done and set it aside to cool for 5 minutes.
7. Remove the loaf from the basket with a little shake and place it on a cooling rack.

NO-YEAST WHOLE-WHEAT SOURDOUGH STARTER

Prep Time: 5 days | Cooking time: 10 minutes | Serves 4

- 1 cup whole-wheat flour, divided
- 1 cup chlorine-free bottled water, at room temperature, divided
- ½ tsp honey

1. Stir together ½ cup of flour, ½ cup of water, and the honey in a large glass bowl with a wooden spoon.
2. Loosely cover the bowl with plastic wrap and place it in a warm area for 5 days, stirring at least twice a day.
3. After 5 days, stir in the remaining ½ cup of flour and ½ cup of water.
4. Cover the bowl loosely again with plastic wrap and place it in a warm area.
5. When the starter has bubbles and foam on top, it is ready to use.
6. Store the starter in the refrigerator in a covered glass jar, and stir it before using.
7. If you use half, replenish the starter with ½ cup flour and ½ cup water.

NO-YEAST BREADS

PUMPKIN QUICK BREAD

Prep time: **2 ½ hours** | Cook time: **10 minutes** | Makes **1 ½ lb loaf**

- 2 ½ cups Light Flour Blend
- 1 ½ cups granulated cane sugar
- ½ cup millet flour
- 1 tbsp baking powder
- 2 tsp psyllium husk flakes or powder
- 2 tsp ground nutmeg
- 2 tsp ground cinnamon
- 1 tsp kosher salt
- 1 tsp ground allspice
- ½ tsp ground cloves
- 15 ounces canned pure pumpkin puree
- ½ cup vegetable or canola oil
- 3 large eggs (beaten)
- ¼ cup water

1. Blend the above-mentioned dry recipe items in a separate bowl, whisk the wet, and scrape them into the bread pan.
2. Spread the dry over the wet components with a spatula.
3. Insert the bread pan into the machine, center it, and lock it in place.
4. Close the lid and choose from the following options: Quick bread/cake cycle; Loaf size: 1 ½ pound; Medium crust; Press Start
5. When the baking is finished, take the bread pan from the machine and place it on a wire cooling rack on its side.
6. Allow for a few minutes in the pan before turning it upside down and sliding the loaf onto the wire rack.
7. Allow the bread to cool before slicing it.

WHITE AND DARK CHOCOLATE TEA CAKE

Prep time: **10 minutes** | Cook time: **20 minutes** | Serves **4**

- 1 cup plain yogurt
- ¼ cup buttermilk
- 2 large eggs
- ¼ cup vegetable oil
- 2 tsp vanilla extract
- ⅔ cup light brown sugar
- 2½ cups unbleached all-purpose flour
- ½ cup unsweetened Dutch-process cocoa powder
- ½ tsp baking powder
- 1½ tsp baking soda
- ½ tsp instant espresso powder
- ¼ tsp salt
- 1 cup white chocolate chips or chunks broken off a bar of white chocolate

1. Place the ingredients in the pan according to the order in the manufacturer's instructions. Set the crust for dark, if your machine offers crust control for this setting, and program for the Quick Bread/Cake cycle; press Start. The batter will be thick. When the machine beeps at the end of the cycle, check the loaf for doneness. The cake is done when it shrinks slightly from the sides of the pan, the sides are dark brown, and the top is firm to a gentle pressure when touched with your finger. A toothpick or metal skewer will come out clean when inserted into the center of the bread.
2. When the bread is done, immediately remove the pan from the machine. Let the bread stand in the pan for 10 minutes before turning it out, right side up, to cool completely on a rack before slicing. Wrap tightly in plastic wrap and store at room temperature.

COLLAGEN KETO GLUTEN-FREE BREAD

Prep time: **5 minutes** | Cook time: **15 minutes** | Serves **12**

- ½ cup collagen protein, unflavored grass-fed
- 6 tbsp. almond flour
- 5 eggs
- 1 tbsp. coconut oil, melted
- 1 tsp baking powder
- 1 tsp xanthan gum
- ¼ tsp Himalayan pink salt

1. Pour all wet ingredients into the bread machine bread pan.
2. Add dry ingredients to the bread machine pan.
3. Set bread machine to the gluten-free setting
4. When the bread is done, remove the bread machine pan from the bread machine.
5. Let cool slightly before transferring to a cooling rack.
6. The bread can be stored for up to 4 days on the counter and for up to 3 months in the freezer.

59

CHAPTER 10

ALMOND QUICK BREAD WITH CARDAMOM

Prep time: **2 ½ hours** | Cook time: **10 minutes** | Makes **1 ½ lb loaf**

- 2½ cups Light Flour Blend
- ½ cup almond flour
- ¼ cup coconut milk powder
- 1 cup granulated cane sugar
- 1 tbsp baking powder
- 1 tbsp psyllium husk flakes or powder
- 2 tsp ground cardamom
- 1 tsp salt
- 1 cup slivered almonds (toasted)
- 3 large eggs (beaten)
- 1 cup water
- ¼ cup vegetable/canola oil

1. Blend the dry (except the slivered almonds) in a large mixing basin.
2. Set aside after adding the almonds.
3. Blend the wet in a 4-cup glass measuring cup and pour into the bread pan.
4. Spread the dry evenly over the wet components using a spatula, totally covering them.
5. Insert the bread pan into the machine, center it, and lock it in place.
6. Close the lid and choose from the following options: quick or cake cycle; 1 ½ pound; medium crust loaf; Press Start.
7. When the baking is finished, take the bread pan from the machine and place it on a wire cooling rack on its side.
8. Allow for a few minutes in the pan before turning it upside down and sliding the loaf onto the wire rack.
9. Allow the bread to cool before slicing it.

CARAMEL APPLE QUICK BREAD

Prep time: **2 ½ hours** | Cook time: **10 minutes** | Makes **1 ½ lb loaf**

- 2½ cups light Flour Blend
- 1 cup granulated cane sugar
- ½ cup teff flour
- ½ cup milk soy powder
- 1 tbsp baking powder
- 1 tbsp psyllium husk flakes or powder
- 1 tsp kosher or fine sea salt
- 3 large eggs (beaten)
- ½ cup applesauce
- ½ cup vegetable oil
- 2 cups grated peeled apples
- 1 ½ cups gluten-free caramel bits

1. Blend the in a large mixing bowl.
2. Whisk together the eggs, applesauce, and oil in a separate large mixing basin.
3. Scrape into the bread pan after stirring in the apples and caramel chunks.
4. Using a spatula, spread the dry evenly over the wet components, totally covering them.
5. Insert the bread pan into the machine, center it, and lock it in place.
6. Close the lid and choose from the following options: quick or cake cycle; 1 ½ pound; medium crust loaf; Press Start.
7. When the baking is finished, take the bread pan from the machine and place it on a wire cooling rack on its side.
8. Allow for a few minutes in the pan before turning it upside down and sliding the loaf onto the wire rack.
9. Allow the bread to cool before slicing it.

NO-YEAST BREADS

TOASTED COCONUT BREAD

Prep time: **10 minutes** | Cook time: **20 minutes** | Serves **4**

- 1¼ cups (about 2½ ounces) shredded unsweetened coconut
- 1⅛ cups half-and-half (regular or fat-free)
- 2 large eggs
- ¼ cup canola oil
- 2 tsp coconut extract
- 1 tsp vanilla extract
- ¾ cup sugar
- 2 cups unbleached all-purpose flour
- 1 tbsp baking powder
- ½ tsp salt

1. Preheat the oven to 350°F.
2. Sprinkle the coconut on an ungreased baking sheet and toast in the oven until lightly browned, about 3 minutes. Transfer immediately to a small bowl and let cool to room temperature.
3. Place the ingredients in the pan according to the order in the manufacturer's instructions, adding the coconut with the dry ingredients. Set the crust for dark, if your machine offers crust control for this setting, and program for the Quick Bread/Cake cycle; press Start. The batter will be thick and smooth. When the machine beeps at the end of the cycle, check the loaf for doneness. The bread is done when it shrinks slightly from the sides of the pan, the sides are dark brown, and the top is firm to a gentle pressure when touched with your finger. A toothpick or metal skewer will come out clean when inserted into the center of the bread.
4. When the bread is done, immediately remove the pan from the machine. Let the bread stand in the pan for 10 minutes before turning it out, right side up, to cool completely on a rack before slicing. Wrap tightly in plastic wrap and store at room temperature.

TROPICAL QUICK BREAD

Prep time: **2 ½ hours** | Cook time: **10 minutes** | Makes **1 ½ lb loaf**

- 2 cups light flour blend/whole-grain flour blend
- 1 cup millet flour
- 2 tsp baking powder
- 1 cup granulated cane sugar
- 1 tbsp psyllium husk flakes or powder
- 1 tsp salt
- ½ cup grated unsweetened coconut
- ½ cup unsweetened coconut milk
- ¼ cup vegetable oil
- 3 large eggs (beaten)
- 1 tsp pure vanilla extract
- 8 ounces canned crushed pineapple (drained)
- ¼ cup coarsely chopped macadamia nuts

1. Blend the dry (except the coconut) in a large mixing basin.
2. Stir in the coconut and toss until all of the dry are nicely coated.
3. Whisk the wet (excluding the pineapple) in a 4-cup glass measuring cup.
4. Pour the mixture into the bread pan after stirring in the pineapple.
5. Spread the dry over the wet components with a spatula.
6. Insert the bread pan into the machine, center it, and lock it in place.
7. Close the lid and choose from the following options: Quick bread/cake cycle; Loaf size: 1 ½ pound; Medium crust; Press Start.
8. Add the macadamia nuts to the mix.
9. Remove the kneading paddle and reshape the bread when you hear the indication for the machine switching from the knead to the bake cycle if your machine has one.
10. If the dough feels sticky, moisten your hands with a little water to aid in reshaping and flattening the top of the loaf.
11. Close the lid and leave the bread alone to finish baking.
12. When the baking is finished, take the bread pan from the machine and place it on a wire cooling rack on its side.
13. Allow for a few minutes in the pan before turning it upside down and sliding the loaf onto the wire rack.
14. Allow the bread to cool before slicing it.

CHAPTER 10

WHOLE WHEAT SODA BREAD

Prep time: **10 minutes** | Cook time: **45 minutes** | Serves **4**

- 1½ cups all purpose flour
- 2 cups bread flour
- 1 tsp sugar
- 1 tsp salt
- 2 cups buttermilk
- 1½ tsp olive oil
- ½ cup evaporated or full cream milk
- 1 tsp baking soda

1. Preparing the Ingredients. Combine all the dry ingredients. Mix all the wet ingredients.
2. Place in the bread pan in the liquid-dry layering.
3. Put the pan in the Hamilton Beach bread machine.
4. Set the loaf size and choose medium for the crust color.
5. Select the Bake cycle. Press the menu and choose Rapid Whole Wheat. This bread has no yeast and does not need the rising and proofing time. Press Start. Set the rapid bake time to 45 minutes.
6. Remove the pan from the bread machine immediately. Cool in the pan completely.

CITRUS CRANBERRY BREAD

Prep time: **1 ½ hour** | Cook time: **10 minutes** | Makes **1,5 lb loaf**

- ¾ cup milk
- ¾ cup sugar
- ⅔ cup melted butter
- 2 eggs
- ¼ tsp ground nutmeg
- ¼ cup freshly squeezed orange juice
- 1 tbsp orange zest
- 1½ tsp baking powder
- 1 tsp pure vanilla extract
- ½ tsp salt
- 2¼ cups all-purpose flour
- 1 cup sweetened dried cranberries
- ½ tsp baking soda

1. Combine the (milk, sugar, butter, eggs, orange juice, zest, and vanilla) in your bread machine.
2. Press Start after programming the machine for quick or rapid bread.
3. In a medium mixing basin, combine the flour, cranberries, baking powder, baking soda, salt, and nutmeg while the wet are mixed.
4. When the machine indicates that the initial quick mixing is complete, add the dry.
5. Remove the bucket from the machine after the loaf is done.
6. Allow 5 minutes for the bread to cool.
7. Remove the loaf from the bucket with a little shake and place it on a cooling rack.

ANADAMA QUICK BREAD

Prep time: **10 minutes** | Cook time: **20 minutes** | Serves **4**

- 1⅔ cups buttermilk
- ½ cup light molasses
- ¼ cup vegetable oil
- 1 large egg
- 1¼ cups whole wheat flour
- 1¼ cups unbleached all-purpose flour
- ½ cup fine or medium-grind yellow cornmeal, preferably stone-ground
- 2 tsp baking powder
- 1 tsp baking soda
- 1 tsp salt

1. Place the ingredients in the pan according to the order in the manufacturer's instructions. Set the crust for dark, if your machine offers crust control for this setting, and program for the Quick Bread/Cake cycle; press Start. The batter will be thick and smooth. When the machine beeps at the end of the cycle, check the loaf for doneness. The bread is done when it shrinks slightly from the sides of the pan, the sides are dark brown, and the top is firm to a gentle pressure when touched with your finger. A toothpick or metal skewer will come out clean when inserted into the center of the bread.
2. When the bread is done, immediately remove the pan from the machine. Let the bread stand in the pan for 10 minutes before turning it out, right side up, to cool completely on a rack. Brush the top with some melted butter. Wrap tightly in plastic wrap and store at room temperature.

CHAPTER 11: BREAD FROM AROUND THE WORLD

CHAPTER 11

RUSSIAN RYE BREAD

Prep time: **5 minutes** | Cook time: **3 hours** | Serves **12**

- 1 ¼ cups warm water
- 1 ¾ cups rye flour
- 1 ¾ cups whole wheat flour
- 2 tbsp malt (or beer kit mixture)
- 1 tbsp molasses
- 2 tbsp white vinegar
- 1 tsp salt
- ½ tbsp coriander seeds
- ½ tbsp caraway seeds
- 2 tsp active dry yeast

1. Mix dry ingredients together in a bowl, except for yeast.
2. Add wet ingredients to bread pan first; top with dry ingredients.
3. Make a well in the center of the dry ingredients and add the yeast.
4. Press Basic bread cycle, choose medium crust color, and press Start.
5. Remove from bread pan and allow to cool on a wire rack before serving.

ITALIAN SEMOLINA BREAD

Prep time: **3 ½ hours** | Cook time: **10 minutes** | Makes **1 ½ lb loaf**

- 1 cup water
- 1 tsp salt
- 2½ tbsp butter
- 2½ tsp sugar
- 2¼ cups flour
- ⅓ cups semolina
- 1½ tsp dry yeast

1. Fill your bread machine halfway with all of the and follow the manufacturer's directions carefully.
2. Set your bread machine's program to Italian Bread/Sandwich mode and medium crust type.
3. Start by pressing the START button.
4. Wait till the cycle is finished.
5. When the loaf is done (when the bake cycle ends), remove it from the bucket and set it aside to cool down for a few minutes.
6. To remove the bread, gently shake the bucket.
7. Placed the bread on a wire rack to cool before slicing and serving.

MOROCCAN KHOBZ

Prep time: **10 minutes** | Cook time: **3 hours** | Serves **6-8**

- 1 cup warm water
- 2 ¼ tsp instant yeast
- 3 cups all-purpose flour
- 1 tsp salt
- 1 tbsp olive oil
- 1 tsp sesame seeds

1. Combine warm water and yeast in bread machine pan. Let stand for 5 minutes.
2. Add flour, salt, and olive oil.
3. Select the dough cycle.
4. Once dough is ready, shape into an oval loaf and place on a baking sheet sprinkled with sesame seeds.
5. Let rise until doubled, then bake in a preheated 400°F oven for 25-30 minutes.

BREAD FROM AROUND THE WORLD

CRUSTY FRENCH BREAD

Prep time: **3 hours 35 minutes** | Cook time: **5 minutes** | Serves **one loaf**

- 1 tsp of instant yeast
- 1 ½ tsp of sugar
- 1 cup of lukewarm water
- 1 ½ tsp salt
- 1 ½ tsp of butter
- 3 cups of bread flour

Glaze:

- 1 tsp of water
- 1 egg white

1. Add all the required to the bread machine as per your machine's suggested order.
2. Select the dough cycle. Adjust the dough's consistency after 5 to 10 minutes by adding 1 tbsp of water at a time for very dry dough or 1 tbsp of flour if it's too sticky.
3. It should pull away after sticking to the sides.
4. When the machine beeps and the dough is done, take it out on a clean, floured surface. Shape into cylinder shape loaves. Shape into French bread.
5. Place the loaves in oiled baking pans. Cover with a towel and let it rise in a warm place.
6. Let the oven preheat to 425 F. make the glaze by mixing water with egg.
7. Coat the loaf's surface with a glaze.
8. Make cuts onto the dough surface.
9. Bake in the oven for 20 minutes.
10. Lower the oven's temperature to 350 F, bake for 5 to 10 minutes more or until golden brown.
11. Check the bread's internal temperature. It should be 195 F.
12. Cool slightly and Serve fresh.

GERMAN BUTTER CAKE

Prep time: **10 minutes** | Cook time: **2 hour 25 minutes** | Serves **12 to 16**

- 2 tsp active dry yeast
- ¼ cup sugar
- 2 ¼ cups all-purpose flour
- 1 tsp salt
- 1 cup whole milk, lukewarm
- 1 egg yolk
- 1 tbsp butter, softened

For the Topping:

- 3 tbsp butter, cold
- ½ cup almonds, sliced
- ⅓ cup sugar

1. Add all of the dough ingredients to the bread maker pan.
2. Press Dough cycle and Start.
3. Grease a 10-inch springform pan; when the dough cycle is finished, pat the dough into the pan.
4. Prepare the topping by cutting the butter into - inch squares and place them sporadically over the surface of the dough, slightly pushing each into the dough.
5. Sprinkle with almond slices, then sprinkle evenly with sugar.
6. Cover with a towel and let stand in a warm place for 30 minutes.
7. Preheat an oven to 375°F.
8. Bake for 20 to 25 minutes or until golden brown.
9. Let cool 10 minutes in pan on cooling rack and serve warm!

CHAPTER 11

RUSSIAN BLACK BREAD

Prep time: 5 minutes | Cook time: 3 hours | Serves 1

- 1 ¼ cups dark rye flour
- 2 ½ cups unbleached flour
- 1 tsp instant coffee
- 2 tbsp unsweetened cocoa powder
- 1 tbsp whole caraway seeds
- ½ tsp dried minced onion
- ½ tsp fennel seeds
- 1 tsp sea salt
- 2 tsp active dry yeast
- 1 ⅓ cups water, at room temperature
- 1 tsp sugar
- 1 ½ tbsp dark molasses
- 1 ½ tbsp apple cider vinegar
- 3 tbsp vegetable oil

1. Mix dry ingredients together in a bowl, except for yeast.
2. Add wet ingredients to bread pan first; top with dry ingredients.
3. Make a well in the center of the dry ingredients and add the yeast.
4. Select Basic bread cycle, medium crust color, and press Start.
5. Let cool for 15 minutes before slicing.

GERMAN PUMPERNICKEL

Prep time: 10 minutes | Cook time: 2 hours | Serves : 8-10

- 2 cups whole wheat flour
- 1 cup rye flour
- 1 tsp instant yeast
- 1 tsp caraway seeds
- 1 tsp salt
- 1 cup water
- 1 tbsp molasses

1. Combine dry ingredients in the bread machine pan.
2. Add water and molasses.
3. Select the dough cycle.
4. Once dough is ready, shape into a loaf and place in a greased bread pan.
5. Let rise until doubled and bake according to bread machine instructions.

JAPANESE MILK BREAD

Prep time: 10 minutes | Cook time: 3 hours | Serves : 8-10

- 1 cup whole milk
- ¼ cup granulated sugar
- 2 ¼ tsp instant yeast
- 3 ½ cups bread flour
- 1 ½ tsp salt
- ¼ cup unsalted butter, softened

1. Warm milk and sugar until sugar dissolves. Let cool slightly.
2. Add yeast to milk mixture and let stand for 5 minutes.
3. Combine flour and salt in bread machine pan.
4. Add yeast mixture and butter to flour mixture.
5. Select the dough cycle.
6. Once dough is ready, shape into a loaf and place in a greased loaf pan.
7. Let rise until doubled, then bake in a preheated 350°F (175°C) oven for 30-35 minutes.

BREAD FROM AROUND THE WORLD

PORTUGUESE SWEET BREAD

Prep time: **10 minutes** | Cook time: **20 minutes** | Serves **4**

- ¾ cup evaporated milk
- ⅓ cup plus 1 tbsp water
- 2 large eggs
- 4 tbsp butter, melted
- ½ tsp lemon extract
- 1 tbsp plus 1 tsp vanilla extract or vanilla powder
- 3¾ cups bread flour
- ½ cup light brown sugar
- 1½ tbsp instant potato flakes
- 1 tbsp gluten
- 2 tsp salt
- 3 tsp SAF yeast or 1 tbsp plus ½ tsp bread machine yeast

1. Place all the ingredients in the pan according to the order in the manufacturer's instructions. Set crust on dark and program for the Basic or Sweet Bread cycle; press Start. (This recipe is not suitable for use with the Delay Timer.)
2. When the baking cycle ends, immediately remove the bread from the pan and place it on a rack. Let cool to room temperature before slicing.

GREEK EASTER BREAD

Prep time: **20 minutes** | Cook time: **3 hours** | Serves **12**

- ⅔ cup fresh butter
- 1 cup milk
- 1 cup sugar
- 1 tsp mastic
- ½ tsp salt
- 1 package active dry yeast
- 3 eggs
- 5 cups strong yellow flour
- 1 egg, for brushing blended with 1 tsp water

1. Heat milk and butter until melted in a saucepan; do not boil. Add to bread maker pan.
2. Add sugar and mastic to a food processor and blend; add to bread maker pan.
3. Add remaining ingredients.
4. Set Dough cycle and press Start; leave dough to rise one hour after cycle.
5. Shape into 2 loaves, cover, and leave to rise for 50 more minutes.
6. Baste with egg wash.
7. Bake at 320°F for 30 to 40 minutes or until golden brown.
8. Transfer to cooling rack for 15 minutes before serving.

AUSTRALIAN DAMPER

Prep time: **5 minutes** | Cook time: **1 hour** | Serves **4-6**

- 2 cups self-rising flour
- 1 cup buttermilk
- ¼ cup butter, cold and cubed

1. Combine flour and butter in bread machine pan.
2. Add buttermilk.
3. Select the dough cycle.
4. Once dough is ready, shape into a round loaf and place on a hot griddle or cast iron skillet.
5. Cook for 20-25 minutes, or until golden brown.

CHAPTER 11

INDIAN NAAN

Prep time: **10 minutes** | Cook time: **2 hours** | Serves : **6-8**

- 1 cup warm water
- 2 ¼ tsp instant yeast
- 2 ½ cups all-purpose flour
- 1 tsp salt
- 2 tbsp plain yogurt
- 2 tbsp melted butter
- 1 clove garlic, minced
- Fresh cilantro, chopped (for topping)

1. Combine warm water and yeast in bread machine pan. Let stand for 5 minutes.
2. Add flour, salt, yogurt, and melted butter.
3. Select the dough cycle.
4. Once dough is ready, divide into small balls.
5. Roll out each ball into an oval shape.
6. Brush with melted butter and sprinkle with garlic and cilantro.
7. Cook on a hot griddle or skillet until golden brown and puffed up.

ITALIAN PINE NUT BREAD

Prep time: **3 ½ hours** | Cook time: **10 minutes** | Makes **1,5 lb loaf**

- 1 cup+ 2 tbsp water
- 3 cups bread flour
- 2 tbsp sugar
- 1 tsp salt
- 1 ¼ tsp active dry yeast
- ⅓ cup basil pesto
- 2 tbsp flour
- ⅓ cup pine nuts

1. Combine basil pesto and 2 tbsp flour in a small container and stir until thoroughly combined.
2. Stir in the pine nuts thoroughly.
3. Combine the water, bread flour, sugar, salt, and yeast in the bread machine pan.
4. Select the basic setting, and then medium crust, and then press the start button.
5. Just before the final kneading cycle, add the basil pesto mixture.
6. Remove the loaf pan from the machine after the loaf is done.
7. Allow 10 minutes for cooling.
8. Cut into slices and serve.

APPENDIX 1: MEASUREMENT CONVERSION CHART

MEASUREMENT CONVERSION CHART

VOLUME EQUIVALENTS (DRY)

US STANDARD	METRIC (APPROXIMATE)
1/8 teaspoon	0.5 mL
1/4 teaspoon	1 mL
1/2 teaspoon	2 mL
3/4 teaspoon	4 mL
1 teaspoon	5 mL
1 tablespoon	15 mL
1/4 cup	59 mL
1/2 cup	118 mL
3/4 cup	177 mL
1 cup	235 mL
2 cups	475 mL
3 cups	700 mL
4 cups	1 L

WEIGHT EQUIVALENTS

US STANDARD	METRIC (APPROXIMATE)
1 ounce	28 g
2 ounces	57 g
5 ounces	142 g
10 ounces	284 g
15 ounces	425 g
16 ounces (1 pound)	455 g
1.5 pounds	680 g
2 pounds	907 g

VOLUME EQUIVALENTS (LIQUID)

US STANDARD	US STANDARD (OUNCES)	METRIC (APPROXIMATE)
2 tablespoons	1 fl.oz.	30 mL
1/4 cup	2 fl.oz.	60 mL
1/2 cup	4 fl.oz.	120 mL
1 cup	8 fl.oz.	240 mL
1 1/2 cup	12 fl.oz.	355 mL
2 cups or 1 pint	16 fl.oz.	475 mL
4 cups or 1 quart	32 fl.oz.	1 L
1 gallon	128 fl.oz.	4 L

TEMPERATURES EQUIVALENTS

FAHRENHEIT (F)	CELSIUS (C) (APPROXIMATE)
225 °F	107 °C
250 °F	120 °C
275 °F	135 °C
300 °F	150 °C
325 °F	160 °C
350 °F	180 °C
375 °F	190 °C
400 °F	205 °C
425 °F	220 °C
450 °F	235 °C
475 °F	245 °C
500 °F	260 °C

APPENDIX 2: THE DIRTY DOZEN AND CLEAN FIFTEEN

The Dirty Dozen and Clean Fifteen

The Environmental Working Group (EWG) is a nonprofit, nonpartisan organization dedicated to protecting human health and the environment Its mission is to empower people to live healthier lives in a healthier environment. This organization publishes an annual list of the twelve kinds of produce, in sequence, that have the highest amount of pesticide residue-the Dirty Dozen-as well as a list of the fifteen kinds ofproduce that have the least amount of pesticide residue-the Clean Fifteen.

THE DIRTY DOZEN

- The 2016 Dirty Dozen includes the following produce. These are considered among the year's most important produce to buy organic:

Strawberries	Spinach
Apples	Tomatoes
Nectarines	Bell peppers
Peaches	Cherry tomatoes
Celery	Cucumbers
Grapes	Kale/collard greens
Cherries	Hot peppers

- The Dirty Dozen list contains two additional itemskale/collard greens and hot peppers-because they tend to contain trace levels of highly hazardous pesticides.

THE CLEAN FIFTEEN

- The least critical to buy organically are the Clean Fifteen list. The following are on the 2016 list:

Avocados	Papayas
Corn	Kiw
Pineapples	Eggplant
Cabbage	Honeydew
Sweet peas	Grapefruit
Onions	Cantaloupe
Asparagus	Cauliflower
Mangos	

- Some of the sweet corn sold in the United States are made from genetically engineered (GE) seedstock. Buy organic varieties of these crops to avoid GE produce.

APPENDIX 3: INDEX

A

almond extract 54
apple cider vinegar 41, 66
apricots 19, 22
aquafaba 13, 47

B

beer 13
beetroot 43, 46
bourbon 58
bread flour 11, 21
bread machine yeast 9, 11
buttermilk 17, 24, 36

C

canola oil 17
caraway seeds 22, 64, 66
chia seeds 11, 37
chickpea flour 38
chili flakes 43
chocolate chips 52, 59
cilantro 68
coconut extract 61
coconut flour 41
coconut milk powder 60
coffee 66
coriander seeds 64
cornmeal 58
cornstarch 38
cranberries 48, 52, 62

D

dried fruits 49
dry yeast 22

F

flax meal 34

flax seed 32, 40

G

gluten 9, 11, 15, 17, 19, 67
guar gum 34

L

lemon rind 28
Light Flour Blend 21, 48
light molasses 19

M

malt extract 30
maple syrup 19
margarine 24
mastic 67
molasses 19

N

nutmeat 42
nut oil 24, 42

O

oat bran 13
oatmeal 13
onion flakes 53
orange juice 48
orange zest 50
oregano 41

P

pepperoni 30
pineapple 24, 47, 54
pizza 30
poppy seed 22, 28
potato buds 36
potato flake 15

potato starch 34, 37, 38
psyllium husk flakes 48, 59, 60, 61
pumpkin 47
pumpkin pie spice 47

R

raisins 34, 40
rosemary leaves 12
rye flour 22

S

SAF yeast 9, 11, 13, 15, 17, 19, 22, 27, 36, 49, 55
salami 56
self-risinggluten-free flour 24
semolina 64
sesame seeds 18
Silk Soy Original 12
sour cream 52
sourdough starter 21, 22, 24, 25
strawberries 49
sugar cubes 55
sunflower oil 40
sunflower seeds 40

V

vanilla extract 59
vegetable oil 15

W

walnut 13, 44
walnut oil 22
wheat bran 9
wheat flour 17
white bread flour 13

71

Hey there!

Wow, can you believe we've reached the end of this culinary journey together? I'm truly thrilled and filled with joy as I think back on all the recipes we've shared and the flavors we've discovered. This experience, blending a bit of tradition with our own unique twists, has been a journey of love for good food. And knowing you've been out there, giving these dishes a try, has made this adventure incredibly special to me.

Even though we're turning the last page of this book, I hope our conversation about all things delicious doesn't have to end. I cherish your thoughts, your experiments, and yes, even those moments when things didn't go as planned. Every piece of feedback you share is invaluable, helping to enrich this experience for us all.

I'd be so grateful if you could take a moment to share your thoughts with me, be it through a review on Amazon or any other place you feel comfortable expressing yourself online. Whether it's praise, constructive criticism, or even an idea for how we might do things differently in the future, your input is what truly makes this journey meaningful.

This book is a piece of my heart, offered to you with all the love and enthusiasm I have for cooking. But it's your engagement and your words that elevate it to something truly extraordinary.

Thank you from the bottom of my heart for being such an integral part of this culinary adventure. Your openness to trying new things and sharing your experiences has been the greatest gift.

Catch you later,

Elizabeth E. Wright

Printed in Great Britain
by Amazon